NOOR

NOOR

◆≫ A CHAMPION THOROUGHBRED'S ≪◆
UNLIKELY JOURNEY *from* CALIFORNIA *to* KENTUCKY

MILTON C. TOBY

Published by The History Press
Charleston, SC 29403
www.historypress.net

Copyright © 2012 by Milton C. Toby
All rights reserved

First published 2012

ISBN 978.1.60949.561.9

Library of Congress CIP data applied for

Notice: The information in this book is true and complete to the best of our knowledge. It is offered without guarantee on the part of the author or The History Press. The author and The History Press disclaim all liability in connection with the use of this book.

All rights reserved. No part of this book may be reproduced or transmitted in any form whatsoever without prior written permission from the publisher except in the case of brief quotations embodied in critical articles and reviews.

Contents

Acknowledgements 7
Introduction 11

PART I: A MIRACLE YEAR
1. Changing of the Guard 19
2. Burley and the Pumper 27
3. Great Expectations 39
4. The Big 'Cap 51
5. "Greatest Race I've Ever Seen!" 61
6. The Fastest Track in the Country 73
7. Horse of the Year? 83
8. Retirement 103

PART II: OLD FRIENDS
9. Loma Rica 109
10. Old Friends 135

Notes 145
Sources 157
About the Author 159

Acknowledgements

There's an irony inherent in the lengthy process that develops the germ of an idea into a finished book. The writing itself is a very solitary endeavor, and an author facing a blank sheet of paper—or more likely these days, a keyboard and a blank computer screen—faces it alone. But other people are involved at every stage, and their involvement is essential to the success of the project.

Topping that list of people, lengths in front of everyone else, is Charlotte Farmer.

It's often said that a book would not have been possible without the help of a spouse, a friend, a colleague, a hero—someone. That sentiment is literally true when it comes to Charlotte Farmer and the story of Noor. Charlotte championed the preservation and recognition of Noor's burial site in Northern California singlehandedly for a while. Later, when the prospect of commercial development threatened the site and her objective shifted to locating Noor's remains and moving them to a more secure location, she began recruiting others to help. Both friends and strangers alike usually found it impossible to say "No" to one of Charlotte's requests.

Ariadne Delon Scott summed up what everyone I talked with said of Charlotte: "Without her, none of this would have happened."

They were right.

She provided invaluable assistance with research for this project, and she was kind enough to share her address book when I needed contacts to add an important bit of information to the story. She worked tirelessly without any

ACKNOWLEDGEMENTS

sort of personal agenda, and her only request was that the book would, in some way, benefit Old Friends, the Thoroughbred retirement farm in Central Kentucky where Noor was reburied last summer. To that end, a portion of the proceeds from the sales of this book will be donated to Old Friends.

Cathy Schenck in particular, and the staff at the Keeneland Library in general, provided invaluable reference material and assistance. The Keeneland Library is home to what must be the most complete archive of the *Daily Racing Form* on the planet, along with an astounding collection of books, magazines and photographs related to Thoroughbred racing. By its own count, the library houses "more than 10,000 volumes, 1,500 videocassettes, 225,000 photo negatives and 3,000 files containing thousands of newspaper clippings." The prospect of compiling any sort of historical narrative about the sport without utilizing the resources of the Keeneland Library would be daunting.

I also had access to reference material and photographs in the files of the *Thoroughbred Times* and the *Blood-Horse*. Special thanks to Mary Simon, who took time from her real work to help locate articles and images. And because of a years-long research project by Charlotte Farmer, I had easy access to the *Los Angeles Times*, the *San Francisco Examiner* and the *San Francisco Chronicle*, all without a trip to the West Coast.

Others who deserve special mention include Edward Kip Hannan and Bill Mochon.

Kip's official job title is supervisor of production operations in the Television Department at Betfair Hollywood Park in California. Informally, though, he spends an extraordinary amount of time locating and restoring the photographic history of racing in Southern California. He provided restored copies of newsreel, promotional and film patrol versions of the 1950 Hollywood Gold Cup; a stack of eight-by-ten glossy photographs; negatives that may not have seen the light of day for more than sixty years; and an audio recording of the actual radio broadcast of the race. You can see a sample of Kip's work, a short newsreel clip of the Gold Cup and images of Noor looking hale and hearty after his retirement, on YouTube (http://www.youtube.com/watch?v=ITp4K8o55kI). The image of Noor on the cover of this book was reproduced from one of the negatives unearthed by Kip. It's possible that this image was never printed and is being seen for the first time.

Bill has been photographing at West Coast tracks for decades. When he discovered, by accident, that thousands of photographic negatives from racing's golden age were being tossed out in the trash, he stepped in and rescued them. Bill Mochon Archival Photo is the repository for the negatives, from which he generously provided prints documenting the Santa Anita Handicap.

Acknowledgements

Thankfully, Kip and Bill understand that a photograph really is worth a thousand words and that once historical images are lost, they're gone forever.

Archaeologists Erin Dwyer and Denise Jaffke worked on the dig at Loma Rica. Denise shared her photographs of the excavation, and they both helped me understand how you locate and exhume the remains of a horse that was buried almost forty years ago. It's not as easy as it sounds.

Several members of Burley Parke's family, including Gary Parke and Don Bosley, shared valuable recollections of their father. Thanks, Gary, for the nifty hat emblazoned with Noor's name and the GPS coordinates for his burial site at Old Friends.

Dan Silvestri, owner of Impact Photography in Lexington, Kentucky, helped with restoration of some of the negatives I received from Kip Hannan, including the photograph on the cover.

Michael Blowen, owner of Old Friends, spent an afternoon talking about the retirement farm and how Noor's remains ultimately found a final resting place in Georgetown, Kentucky.

Veteran turf writer Jon White shared a story about Noor's jockey, John Longden, and pointed me in the direction of other sources.

Will McKay, my editor at The History Press, had faith in the idea that the story of a champion Thoroughbred racehorse that hardly anyone remembered and an energetic woman in California who resurrected his memory was worthy of a book. Everyone at the Charleston, South Carolina publishing house has been wonderful to work with from start to finish.

Finally, the support from my wife, Roberta, was unwavering. The only thing more difficult than actually writing a book might be living with someone who is!

Introduction

A few minutes after sunrise on a foggy West Texas highway, a Greyhound bus piloted by a substitute driver rushing to make up lost time slammed head-on into an automobile driven by golfer Ben Hogan. In the split second before impact, Hogan flung himself across the passenger seat to protect his wife, Valerie. The instinctive decision saved Hogan's life, but the Cadillac was demolished in the collision, and the golfer sustained serious injuries. Complications set in early on, and for a time it was not at all clear whether Hogan would ever play golf again.[1]

The year was 1949, and one of the world's best golfers was out of action for the foreseeable future, maybe forever.

Another sports icon of postwar America, the Thoroughbred racehorse Citation, Triple Crown winner and Horse of the Year, already was on the sidelines at the time of Hogan's accident. After winning the 1948 Pimlico Special in a walkover when no other trainer could be enticed to run a horse against him, Citation was shipped to California to prepare for an assault the next year on two major records. Stymie's career earnings mark of $918,485 was the first objective. Becoming Thoroughbred racing's first millionaire was the second.

Achieving either goal was far from a sure thing, even for a stellar horse like Citation, but neither objective was outside the realm of possibility. California tracks offered more than their share of lucrative opportunities, including the rich Santa Anita Handicap and the Hollywood Gold Cup. For a stable with Calumet's history of winning just about everything in sight, along with the general prejudice held against West Coast horses by the eastern elite, the rich California purses must have looked like low-hanging fruit, ready to be picked.

As often happens, things didn't go exactly as planned.

Citation was coming off a hard three-year-old campaign, but he appeared to be fit and sound and ready to race when trainer Jimmy Jones and the Calumet string arrived in California. Rather than give the colt some time off, which he probably needed, Jones accepted an unexpected invitation from a close friend, Gene Mori, to run Citation in the 1948 Tanforan Handicap. Mori recently had purchased the Tanforan track, and he needed a box office draw for the Northern California track's premier event. It would be a tuneup for racing at Santa Anita and quick money for Citation.

"Good horses make racing fans," Mori told Jones, "and there is no better horse than Citation. Furthermore, our $50,000 Tanforan Handicap looks like an easy race."[2]

The Calumet colt fit the bill perfectly, Jones thought, and the winner's share of the purse would move Citation even closer to Stymie in the money race. He said OK.

Citation dutifully won a prep race in the mud on December 3 (his fourteenth consecutive win) and the Tanforan Handicap by five lengths a little over a week later (number fifteen in a row, as expected). The victories boosted Citation's earnings for the year to a record $709,470, but there was a hefty price to pay. The colt soon developed an osselet—a seriously enlarged joint—in his left front ankle. The stress injury was treated, and Citation was put away for all of the 1949 season.

"We went to the well once too often," Jones lamented afterward.[3]

Citation's career earnings totaled $865,150, tantalizingly close to Stymie's mark of $918,485. But with the Calumet star out of action, Stymie's earnings record was safe for a while longer.

The year-long layoffs imposed on Hogan and Citation by their injuries set up 1950 as a much-anticipated year for comebacks. One turned out better than anyone could have predicted given the long odds against a successful return; the other, not so much.

Introduction

Ben Hogan returned to competitive golf in January 1950, finishing second to Sam Snead in a playoff for the Los Angeles Open. Five months later, at the historic Merion Golf Club outside Philadelphia, Hogan put the crowning touches on his miraculous comeback, finishing tied for the lead in the U.S. Open after seventy-two holes and winning in an eighteen-hole playoff the next day. Hogan managed the exhausting feat on legs swathed in elastic bandages, walking eighteen holes on Thursday, eighteen holes on Friday, thirty-six holes on Saturday and an added eighteen holes in the Sunday playoff. His legion of fans was ecstatic, and any doubts about the Hogan legend were erased.

Citation didn't fare so well. He won a six-furlong allowance race at Santa Anita his first time out in more than a year, on January 11, 1950, for his sixteenth consecutive victory. Factoring in Citation's year-long layoff in 1949, the Calumet star hadn't been defeated since April 1948.

The streak was broken two weeks later when Citation unexpectedly lost a six-furlong handicap to Miche. The race was aptly named the La Sopresa Handicap (Spanish for "the surprise"), and Jimmy Jones attributed the loss to the 16-pound spread in weight carried by Citation (130 pounds) and Miche (114).

"Weight brings horses together," Jones said after the race.[4]

It would become a common lament for Citation's supporters during the next few months.

Citation lost to stablemate Ponder in his next race, the San Antonio Handicap. It was the first time the horse ever lost two races in a row, and the defeat was a harbinger of things to come. Jones next saddled Citation for the rich Santa Anita Handicap, a $100,000 race that had been one of Calumet's principal goals for the horse before the injury in 1948. The Big 'Cap is where the wheels really came off the Calumet express.

Noor,[5] an Irish-bred, English-foaled horse owned by Charles S. Howard, upset Citation in the Santa Anita Handicap and then handed the Calumet star three more defeats, in the San Juan Capistrano, Forty Niners' and Golden Gate Handicaps. The handsome Irish import set three world records in the process, and by summer, Noor had established his credentials as the best handicap horse—maybe the best horse in any division—in the country.

Unable to beat Noor, Citation was shipped east. He already had eclipsed Stymie's career earnings mark, and he became racing's first million-dollar winner in 1951.

Noor was retired from racing after winning the richest race of the year, the $100,000 Hollywood Gold Cup, in December 1950. He clearly was

INTRODUCTION

the year's best older horse and arguably would have been named Horse of the Year if the Gold Cup had been run *before* the championship voting was conducted instead of afterward. The Hollywood Gold Cup had probably the strongest field of any race that year. Among the horses Noor defeated in that race was Hill Prince, the year's champion three-year-old male and overall winner on Horse of the Year ballots.

The passage of time, inexplicably, has not been kind to Noor, despite his remarkable string of wins over one of the best horses ever to race.[6] It could be that he simply needed a better press agent.

Charles Howard was a tireless promoter of Seabiscuit when that horse raced during the post-Depression years, and the press elevated the horse to the status of a national hero. By Noor's year, 1950, Howard was seriously ill and unable to court the media as he had done on behalf of Seabiscuit. He died midway through the year, leaving Noor a rising star in California but without the national attention he deserved.

There also was a certain stigma associated with beating one of the best horses ever to race. Citation got good press coverage when he won because he was supposed to win; when Citation lost to Noor, however, it was so unexpected that reporters focused on the loser rather than on the winner.

Critics of Noor argued that the Howard runner benefited from a significant break in the weights in the Santa Anita and San Juan Capistrano Handicaps and that Citation at five was not the same horse he had been at three. Even trainer Jimmy Jones dismissed Citation's losses to Noor with an excuse.

"He was a true champion and a great horse," Jones said of Citation after the trainer's retirement from Calumet Farm, "up until he sustained his injury at Tanforan at the end of his career as a 3-year-old. Citation should not be judged by his races after that time; he was merely trying to reach a goal of being the first winner of one million dollars, racing on an injured ankle. Possibly, he should have been retired earlier, but he was after a record and he attained that goal."[7]

Conveniently forgotten are a couple of important facts. First, Noor won the Golden Gate Handicap in world record time while giving weight to

Citation, and second, the Calumet star still was good enough as a five-year-old to set a world record of his own in the Golden Gate Mile, a race that Noor sat out.

Noor died in 1974 after a moderately successful career at stud. He was buried in the infield of the training track at Loma Rica Ranch in Northern California, where he had been pensioned for several years. No one gave a thought to Noor for decades, until ambitious development plans threatened the Loma Rica property. Charlotte Farmer, an energetic Californian who has never understood the meaning of the word "no," was upset about the lack of respect being shown to Noor, a horse that had played an important role in legitimizing the quality of California racing.

She eventually launched a campaign to locate the horse's unmarked grave—not an easy task after forty years—and move Noor's remains to a suitable burial site where the horse's memory would be safe from encroaching development. She raised money and recruited others to the cause, and like Noor in his races with Citation, she succeeded beyond all expectations.

In August 2011, Noor's remains were driven across country and reburied at Old Friends, a retirement farm for Thoroughbreds in Central Kentucky.

This is Noor's story, and Charlotte's.

PART I
A Miracle Year

1
CHANGING OF THE GUARD

Sergeant Joy knew immediately that something was wrong when he was jarred awake from a sound sleep by some unusual noises coming from Seabiscuit's stall. Joy worked at Charles S. Howard's sprawling Ridgewood Ranch, a couple hours north of San Francisco, and he spent his nights in the same barn that housed Seabiscuit. The horse had appeared normal when Howard checked on him the previous evening, but hours later, he was in obvious distress. When the groom reached the stall, he found Seabiscuit down in the straw, struggling to get to his feet. He called Dr. John W. Britton, who did the veterinary work at Ridgewood, but the stricken horse was beyond help. Seabiscuit died a few minutes after Dr. Britton arrived, victim of an apparent heart attack.[8]

Howard always thought of Seabiscuit as much a "member of the family"[9] as a champion Thoroughbred, and he was beset with grief over the loss of the horse.

"I never dreamed the old boy would go so quickly," he said.[10]

The year was 1947; the date was May 17. Seabiscuit was just seventeen years old, quite young for a Thoroughbred.

What happened after Seabiscuit's death is something of a puzzle.

Perhaps the best-known version of events, popularized in Laura Hillenbrand's bestseller *Seabiscuit: An American Legend*, is that Howard directed that the horse's body be buried at an undisclosed location at Ridgewood, marking the site only with a newly planted oak sapling.[11] The story is credited to a member of the Howard family, who should know, but it seems uncharacteristic behavior for a man who understood and appreciated Seabiscuit's popularity with the public.

Seabiscuit had been immensely popular when he raced, a Depression-era hero during the 1930s, and he attracted a steady stream of visitors to Ridgewood after he was retired. During the first seven months of 1941, when the memory of Seabiscuit still was fresh in everyone's mind, 33,072 people signed the guest book outside the horse's stall. That amounted to an average of more than 150 visitors every day. On some days, there were more than 1,000.[12]

Howard tried his best to accommodate everyone who came to Ridgewood to see Seabiscuit, posting a welcoming sign at the farm entrance and going so far as erecting a small grandstand near the horse's paddock for the visitors. Although it's mere speculation, selecting a more public burial site for Seabiscuit, one that could be visited by the horse's many fans, might have been appropriate under the circumstances.

People mark the passing of time with milestones, and it's tempting to think that Seabiscuit's death marked the end of an era. For Howard, whose sentimental attachment to the horse grew stronger over the years, it probably did. But in reality, the Seabiscuit era for the Howard stable had ended seven years earlier, when the horse edged stablemate Kayak II in the final strides to win the 1940 Santa Anita Handicap.

After finally winning the Big 'Cap, Seabiscuit was retired as the richest Thoroughbred of all time, with career earnings of $437,730. He won thirty-three races over the years, including an epic match against War Admiral, and he ran second or third in thirty-eight others.

The late 1930s were golden years for Howard and his wife, Marcella, and the 1940 Santa Anita Handicap was the zenith. The stable was the nation's leading owner in 1937, with sixty wins and $214,559 in earnings, and again in 1940, when the stable earned $334,120. Howard also ranked second among leading owners in 1939 (with earnings of $246,905) and third in 1938 ($195,925).[13] But those were the years of Seabiscuit and lesser stars like Kayak II, Sorteado, Porter's Cap and Mioland. Everything that followed was a search for another horse that could match the accomplishments of

Seabiscuit and maintain the ascendency of Charles and Marcella Howard's racing fortunes.[14]

Howard's health was failing by the time Seabiscuit died, but he kept looking anyway.

Seabiscuit, as events turned out, proved to be a very difficult act to follow.

Horse of the Year and the leading money winner of all time, Seabiscuit had Man o' War a couple generations back in his pedigree, close enough to attract the attention of anyone who wanted to breed a good horse. He had the race record, the breeding and the intangible star power usually associated with a prominent sire. Whether Seabiscuit could have fulfilled that promise at stud is anybody's guess because Howard did not want to send the horse across country to stand in Kentucky, where he might have attracted the best broodmares. Howard instead wanted to keep Seabiscuit close at hand after the champion was through racing. It was a sentimental decision that hampered his potential as a sire.

Ridgewood was well off the beaten path, and while tourists and fans were eager to make the trek to lay eyes on Seabiscuit, filling the stallion's book with good mares was almost impossible. Any hopes Howard had of the horse becoming the cornerstone of a breeding dynasty at Ridgewood quickly faded. Bred mainly to Howard's own mares, Seabiscuit sired only four stakes winners.[15] Howard's enthusiasm about each new crop of "Little Biscuits" never wavered, even as it became apparent that the horse was not going to be the standout sire the owner wanted him to be. Sea Swallow, Sea Sovereign and a few others turned out to be nice horses, but none of Seabiscuit's offspring came close to approaching their sire's prowess on the racetrack.[16]

If there was going to be a successor to Seabiscuit racing in Howard's red and white silks, it wasn't going to be a homebred.

Howard initially had great success with inexpensive horses, many of which he imported from South America. Champion handicapper Kayak II, winner of the 1938 Santa Anita Handicap, was an Argentine-bred purchased by Howard for $7,500; Sorteado, winner of Argentina's Triple Crown, was a leading handicap horse for Howard before he was injured.[17] It was natural, then, when Howard took an interest in the newly minted Empire City Gold Cup at Belmont Park in New York.

International racing was in its infancy in 1947, the first year the Empire City Gold Cup was run. The race offered a huge purse (the track added $100,000 to nomination and entry fees) and was run at one and five-eighths miles, an uncommonly rich paycheck and a longer-than-usual distance both aimed at attracting horses from Europe. Foreign owners probably liked the race more in theory than in practice, especially considering the arduous trip necessary to compete, and the early foreign contingents were small and unsuccessful.

The inaugural running was won by Stymie, a former claimer that became a champion while racing against some of the best horses of the 1940s. It was Stymie's best year on the track, and his win helped immediately establish the Empire City as a race worth winning.

Triple Crown winner and eventual Horse of the Year Citation frightened away most of his domestic contemporaries for the 1948 running, and only two European horses crossed the Atlantic for the race. One of them was an attractive gray colt named Nathoo, which had won the Irish Derby earlier in the year for his breeder, His Highness Sultan Mahomed Shah, the third Aga Khan. Citation won easily by two lengths under a confident hand ride by jockey Eddie Arcaro; 1947 Belmont Stakes winner Phalanx was second, and Nathoo never was a factor.

The race was Citation's twelfth consecutive victory, and the winner's share of the purse pushed his career earnings over $800,000. It was about this time that Calumet Farm owner Warren Wright began to think seriously that Stymie's earnings record might be vulnerable and that Citation might be the horse to wrest the crown away from the former claimer.

After the Empire City, Prince Aly Khan, son of the Aga Khan, let it be known that Nathoo might be for sale. Prince Aly asked Canadian Charles Spencer to help find a buyer for the colt. Spencer knew Charles Howard was looking for a good horse, and he contacted him. Howard thought Nathoo was a better prospect than his dismal finish in the Empire City showed and said he was interested if the price was right.

It was difficult to not like Nathoo. The horse already had a classic win to his credit, and he had the lineage of a champion, both figuratively and literally.

The Aga Khan's far-flung Thoroughbred empire for decades was (and still is) one of Europe's most successful and prominent breeding and racing operations. Nathoo was in the first crop of foals sired by another of the Aga Khan's horses, Nasrullah, a well-bred but temperamental son of unbeaten

Nearco. Howard liked Nathoo as a racehorse and as a potential sire, a prescient enthusiasm for Nasrullah blood that other American breeders also were beginning to share. Howard's admiration of Nasrullah was well placed. The stallion was on the cusp of becoming one of the twentieth century's most influential sires.

The Aga Khan sold Nasrullah to an Irishman, Joe McGrath, in 1944. Five years later, after a couple of failed negotiations, A.B. (Bull) Hancock put together a syndicate that purchased Nasrullah for a reported $340,000 and brought the stallion to the United States for the 1951 breeding season.[18] Already a prominent sire in England and Ireland, Nasrullah founded a dynasty while standing at Hancock's Claiborne Farm near Paris, Kentucky.

The acquisition of Nasrullah followed several other successful raids on the Aga Khan's stallions by North American breeders. In the late 1930s, Bull Hancock was part of a syndicate that negotiated the controversial purchase of Blenheim II, sire of Triple Crown winner Whirlaway. Sales of Mahmoud and Bahram followed.[19]

Joe Palmer was one of the most erudite writers who ever covered horse racing and also one of the most entertaining to read. He had this to say about the exodus of Nasrullah et al:

> *Immediately after the war some English racing writers attributed the failure of English horses to hold the lists against France to the sparse rationing of wartime, when oats were somewhat too precious to be fed indiscriminately to horses. But as French successes continued, over full-fed English horses, this explanation began to leak. The line now is that too many top English horses were sold and exported to France and America and particularly named were *Nasrullah, *Blenheim II, *Bahram, and *Mahmoud, which is a roundabout way of blaming it all on the Aga Khan, since he bred and sold all of these.*
>
> *All of these names except that of *Mahmoud are in the pedigree of *Noor, probably the best imported horse ever to race in North America. If this statement is challenged, as it may be by someone who remembers *Hourless and *Omar Khayyam, then at least he is the best to race for two seasons in his own area, and then reestablish and, indeed, greatly improve, his form after acclimatization here. There cannot be serious argument after this reservation is made.*[20]

Nasrullah sired ninety-eight stakes winners and led America's sire rankings on four occasions, impressive accomplishments standing alone, but it was through his sons that he achieved even greater prominence. Bold Ruler led the sire list seven consecutive years in the 1960s and then topped the list for an eighth time in 1973, the year his son Secretariat became the first Triple Crown winner since Citation. Other sons of Nasrullah to lead the sire list included T.V. Lark, What a Pleasure, Raja Baba and Triple Crown winner Seattle Slew.

When the *Blood-Horse* magazine assembled a panel of turf writers, breeders and other experts to tackle the difficult and subjective task of identifying one hundred watershed events in racing, the purchase and importation of Nasrullah ranked twenty-third.[21]

An Irish classic winner with an impeccable pedigree, Nathoo figured to command a lofty price. Looking for a second opinion about the horse, Howard got in touch with Rex Ellsworth, a savvy California horseman who would achieve prominence outside his home state when homebred Swaps won the Kentucky Derby a few years later.

What did Ellsworth think of Nathoo? Howard asked.

"I was not trying to sell Howard another horse, or any horse for that matter," Ellsworth said, "but I answered: 'Why buy Nathoo? Noor is a better horse.' I had seen him run third in the English Derby, and he had made a real impression on me."

Although Nathoo was a proven classic winner in Ireland, there was ample reason for Ellsworth to be optimistic about Noor, which boasted a pedigree and race record at least as good as those of his stablemate.

Both horses were sired by Nasrullah, and Noor's dam, Queen of Bagdad, was a well-bred daughter of Epsom Derby winner Bahram. She also was the dam of stakes winner Dilawarji.

Named for the famous, and supposedly cursed,[22] Kohinoor Diamond, Noor won twice as a two-year-old, finishing first in the Bradgate Park Nursery Handicap at Doncaster and the Bretby Nursery Handicap at Newmarket. He won twice more at three, taking the Diomed Stakes at Epsom and the Great Foal Stakes at Newmarket. In the latter, Noor carried the top weight of 133 pounds. Noor also ran third in the 1948 Epsom Derby, won by another of the Aga Khan's horses, My Love. It's difficult to know whether a third-place finish in the Epson Derby trumps a win in the Irish Derby, but John P. Sparkman, who writes about bloodstock matters for the *Thoroughbred Times*, thinks that it does.[23]

"A few days later, Howard called again," Ellsworth said. "He asked if I still thought Noor was the better horse. All I could do then was stick by my earlier statement. Next thing I knew, Howard had bought both Noor and Nathoo."[24]

A Miracle Year

Noor in England prior to the sale to Charles Howard. *Courtesy of* Thoroughbred Times.

Howard never revealed how much he paid for the two-horse package, although at one point he acknowledged to reporters that it was "a lot."[25] There was speculation in the press that Howard got the pair, Noor and Nathoo, for around $175,000, or maybe $200,000, depending on the reporter, with the Irish Derby winner accounting for the majority of that figure. Burley Parke, who trained both horses, guessed that Nathoo and Noor, if purchased separately by Howard, would have been worth at least $120,000 and $40,000, respectively.[26]

In Noor, Howard got a rangy, almost black horse with a small star and one white ankle behind. At seventeen hands, he looked like a horse that would be more comfortable racing over fences rather than on the flat:

> *Noor is a good individual of the typical staying type, standing somewhere over 16 hands, much taller than he is lengthy, and with lean quarters and long muscles of the accepted distance-running variety. He has legs of flat,*

medium-sized bone, his pasterns are right, and the angle of his shoulders suggests the freedom of action to carry weight long distances. Noor's withers would delight a 'chase fan. His barrel is short and the ribs well sprung.

A thin coat that assumes a bright sheen in the sun and a head of almost Arabian modeling indicate Noor's high breeding. There is much of his sire, Nasrullah, about him, except that the latter is a trifle lengthier in the back. Although Nasrullah was said to be rather headstrong in training, Noor is a cheerful runner, responding willingly and gamely whenever Longden asked him to move.[27]

Nathoo never raced in Howard's colors due to a bowed tendon and other problems. The horse also was a failure at stud and turned out to be nothing more than a very expensive disappointment.

Noor, on the other hand, bought sight unseen and almost as an afterthought, more than made up the difference, becoming the star runner Howard was hoping to find. After a decade-long absence, with Noor leading the way as the year's top money winner, the Howard stable was listed among the nation's leaders in 1950.

Noor wasn't the reincarnation of Seabiscuit, never would be, and even Howard refused to elevate the horse to such a pedestal. But the "pig in a poke"[28] turned out to be the next best thing, a champion when the ailing owner desperately wanted one.

2

BURLEY AND THE PUMPER

Tom Smith, the taciturn and idiosyncratic trainer who managed the career of Seabiscuit with consummate skill, stayed with Charles Howard for a while after the stable's star was retired, but a letdown was inevitable. That isn't to say that the stable's fortunes instantly changed for the worse. Howard's red and white colors kept showing up in the winner's circle, just not as often as before and seldom against the best competition.

The owner and trainer finally parted company, amiably enough, in 1943, when Smith was laid up for a year recuperating from back surgery. Howard needed a new trainer, and he knew that Smith, like Seabiscuit, would be difficult to replace.

One of the keys to Howard's phenomenal success selling Buicks over the years was an uncommon knack for hiring good people and then leaving them alone to do their jobs. It was a management philosophy that also worked to great success with Tom Smith. The trainer mapped out campaigns for Howard's horses, and the owner listened, even on those occasions when Smith's plans didn't quite match his own.

After a few false starts, Howard finally settled on trainer Burley Parke as Smith's successor. Howard and Parke already had some history together: the trainer had won the Stars and Stripes and Autumn Handicaps with Howard's Advocator in 1940, the year of Seabiscuit's miraculous victory in the Santa Anita Handicap under the tutelage of Smith.[29]

Howard lost a future Hall of Fame trainer when Tom Smith left the owner's employ. When he hired Burley Parke, the owner managed to find another conditioner destined for a place in the Hall of Fame.

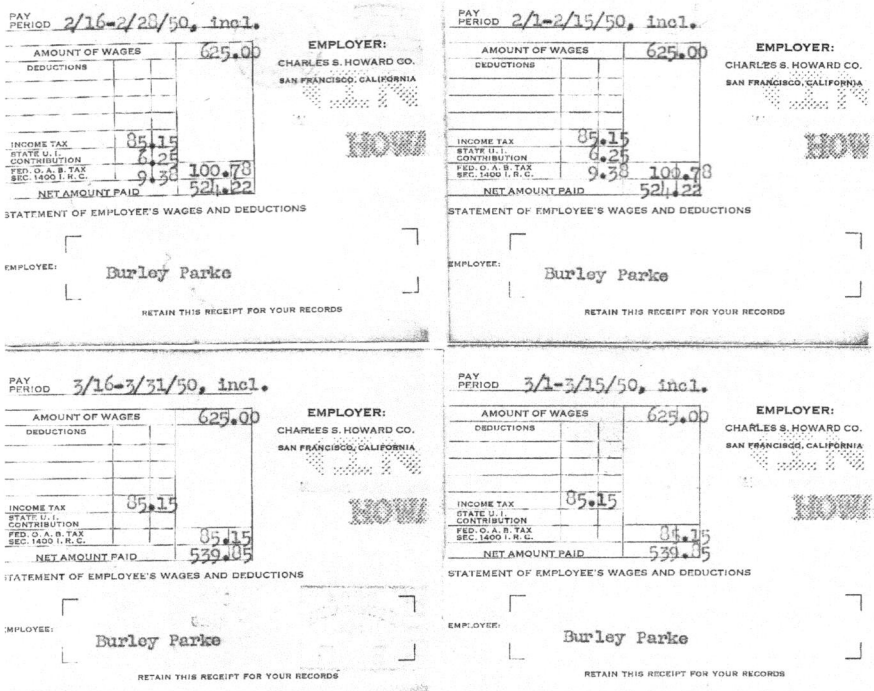

Burley Parke's pay stubs. *Courtesy of the Parke family.*

Parke went to work for Howard in 1947, the year Seabiscuit died. The trainer first laid eyes on Noor and Nathoo either in late 1948 or early 1949, when the pair of pricey Irish-breds joined the Howard stable at Hollywood Park. At first look, Nathoo appeared to be the better of the two. Noor was a nervous horse and a notoriously poor shipper, and he arrived in California in distressingly poor condition. The horse also had ankle problems, which Howard and Parke discovered after the sale was finalized.

"Shortly after his flight from England to New York and subsequent train trip to California, we found he was suffering from green osselets," Howard recalled. "We promptly fired him,[30] turned him out on our rest farm in San Ysidro. We gave him plenty of time, about a year in fact, before placing him back in training. Noor is by Nasrullah and while I purchased him primarily as a stud prospect, we figure he has a couple of years of stakes racing in him before we retire him to the farm."[31]

The horse wouldn't make his first start in Howard's colors for another five months, and he got to the track that quickly only because of Parke's patient handling. Returning Noor to good physical condition and getting him racing sound weren't the real issues; any reasonably competent trainer could have managed those tasks. Settling Noor down and helping acclimatize the horse to an American style of racing, on the other hand, demanded special skill and understanding, traits that Burley Parke had in abundance.

"Noor came to us from the farm with a bad reputation," Parke said. "He was a temperamental character. If you didn't treat him right, there would be trouble."

The *American Racing Manual*'s glowing description of him as a "cheerful runner" notwithstanding, Noor probably inherited a headstrong character from his sire. Nasrullah was well known as a rogue—captions on photographs in *Best Horses of 1943* read, "Nasrullah pretending to be a gentleman," "Nasrullah condescends to pass the post in front in the Chatteris Stakes" and "Nasrullah impersonating a mule"—and there was concern among breeders that he would pass along these traits to his offspring.[32] In Noor's case, this apparently happened. As things turned out, Burley Parke and Noor proved to be a good match.

"The lessons I learned as a youth with Smith, and later the post-graduate work with Burch, enabled me to handle Noor like a good horse should be trained," Burley Parke explained.[33]

"Smith" was Nevada horseman A.E. Smith. "Burch" was legendary trainer Preston Burch.

There isn't a "Parke Family" wing in the Racing Hall of Fame at the National Museum of Racing in Saratoga, but there probably should be. Burley Parke was an extraordinary horseman from a family that produced far more than its share of noteworthy jockeys and trainers.[34] Burley and Ivan both are in the Hall of Fame, and other brothers Vasco, Monte and Chuck also enjoyed successful careers as jockeys and trainers.

There is some dispute about which of the Parke brothers left home first. According to Burley Parke's obituary in the *Blood-Horse*, Burley's older brother Vasco was the first of the Parke boys to feel the lure of the racetrack. Vasco built a local reputation as a successful Roman rider at county fairs near the

Parke family's Idaho home. Roman riders compete in rough-and-tumble races while standing on the backs of their mounts. It's an esoteric pursuit that had no obvious relationship to more traditional jockey race riding, but Vasco's obvious horsemanship skills, courage and small stature nevertheless attracted the attention of bush track trainer Asa E. Smith.

After learning the ropes riding at small tracks in Nevada and California, and a successful season at Tijuana in the 1920s, Vasco retired from the saddle when weight problems finally got the better of him. He didn't sever his ties with racing completely, however, and served as an official at tracks in several states.

On his next trip to Utah, the obituary said, Smith recruited Burley.

In a 1967 interview with the *Daily Racing Form*'s Oscar Otis, however, Burley Parke gave a somewhat different account of things. Parke said that Asa Smith liked Vasco's riding but that the older boy was too heavy to ride as an apprentice. Vasco told Smith that he had a brother who was younger and lighter—Burley—and the trainer took him instead. One thing that the various accounts agree on is that Burley's mother didn't like the idea very much.

"I wanted to go, of course," Parke told Otis, but my mother put up strenuous objections, and only when I promised her that I would not smoke or touch alcoholic beverages until I was 21 would she give her consent. I have never smoked to this day, and it was not until my 40th birthday that I took a drink."

Among the horses Smith was training at the time was Bee's Wing, an inexpensive filly with a penchant for acting up at the start of her races. Smith took his time with Bee's Wing and managed to calm her down, and the filly won a few times with young Burley in the saddle.

"I suppose Bee's Wing was really responsible for the success of the Parke family in racing," Burley said. "If it had not been for Bee's Wing, I might not have made good as a rider, and the others in the family wouldn't have drifted to the Turf. That Smith could really do things with horses."

Burley's talent quickly outpaced the opportunities he had riding for Smith, and his contract was picked up by Hall of Fame trainer Preston Burch. Parke had several successful years with Burch's horses, but as good a jockey as Burley was, his younger brother Ivan was better. Ivan's riding career was cut short due to weight problems, but it was spectacular. He was the country's leading rider twice, once as an apprentice in 1923 and again the next year, and when he retired, he had won on almost one out of every four horses he rode.[35] Unable to make weight for flat races, Ivan had a brief comeback riding in steeplechases, where the scale of weights for jockeys was more forgiving. He was second-leading jump rider in 1931.

Ivan Parke had a second successful career as a trainer. He won the 1945 Kentucky Derby with Fred W. Hooper's Hoop Jr., and he also sent out the outstanding sprinter Olympia. Ivan was elected to the Hall of Fame in 1978.

Burley apprenticed with Burch for a while, where he completed the "graduate work" that would help him sort out Noor's litany of problems years later. It's difficult to imagine a better training ground than time spent watching and learning from a conditioner like Preston Burch. A Hall of Fame trainer in his own right, he occupied the middle position in a three-generation Hall of Fame triumvirate. His father, William P. Burch, enjoyed a career that spanned some sixty years and two centuries. He was a member of the Hall of Fame's inaugural class in 1955. Preston Burch's son, J. Elliott, trained six champions, including four Hall of Fame horses. He followed his grandfather and father into the Hall of Fame in 1980.

Burley Parke sent out his first stakes winner, Timorous, in 1932, but it was not until the early 1940s that he burst onto the national stage as the "Futurity Man."

From 1940 until he started working for Charles Howard in 1947, Parke trained for Charles Marsh, a Chicagoan who owned a succession of outstanding two-year-olds. Parke and Marsh won the Belmont, Arlington, Washington and Breeders' Futurities with Occupation in 1942; the Belmont and Arlington Futurities with Occupy and the Washington Futurity with Jezrabel in 1943; and the Arlington and Washington Futurities with Free For All in 1944—nine major futurities in all. Free For All was an early favorite for the 1945 Kentucky Derby but didn't make it to the race due to an injury. That was the year that Ivan Parke won the Kentucky Derby with Hoop Jr.

Burley and Noor retired from racing together, at the end of the 1950 season, both at the top of their games. Noor was the year's leading money winner, and Parke ranked fifth among the nation's leading trainers. He had thirty winners that year, and horses he saddled won $420,170. The leading trainer in 1950 was Parke's old mentor, Preston Burch.[36]

After nine years hunting, fishing and raising fruit at his Northern California farm, Burley was lured back to the racetrack by a lucrative offer from a newcomer to the sport, Harbor View Farm owner Louis Wolfson. For six years, Burley saddled a succession of outstanding runners for Harbor View, among them juvenile champion Raise a Native (which Parke ranked along with Noor as among the best horses he ever trained) and Horse of the Year and handicap champion Roman Brother.

The Parke brothers, *from left to right*: Monte, Ivan, Chuck, Burley and Vasco. *Courtesy of the Parke family.*

During a career that spanned forty years, Burley was known as much for his patience and soft-spoken demeanor as for his training acumen. His patience with a difficult horse would pay off time after time, from champion Noor to later champions Raise a Native and Roman Brother.

Seabiscuit's regular riders, John ("Red") Pollard and George M. Woolf ("the Iceman"), went their separate ways after the horse was retired in 1940.

Beset by injuries, Red Pollard tried training for a while, but the stress didn't appeal to him.

"It's too hard on the nerves," he explained. "No wonder all trainers have ulcers. As a trainer, I am a barnacle on the wheels of progress."[37]

Pollard eventually returned to a hardscrabble life riding cheap horses at the small tracks on racing's periphery. He died in 1981, following a lengthy illness.

In stark contrast to his close friend, Woolf continued a meteoric rise to the top of his profession until his untimely death in a racing accident in 1946. Woolf reigned as the nation's leading rider in stakes races in 1942–44; he was inducted into the Hall of Fame in 1955. The George Woolf Memorial Jockey Award is presented annually to the rider who best demonstrates high standards of personal and professional conduct.[38]

Basil James was aboard Noor when the horse won his first time out in Charles Howard's silks, in a Tanforan allowance race in October 1949. James continued as Noor's regular rider throughout most of the year and, except for an inopportune twist of fate, likely would have been on the horse for his epic duels with Citation in 1950. Instead, jockey John Longden wound up as Noor's regular rider for all of 1950.

"I remember that Basil James was due to have the mount [on Noor]," Longden recalled years later.

> *But James got set down* [suspended by track stewards for a riding infraction] *and I took over for him. It was an off track. I got left at the gate, so far back that I didn't see much point in doing anything with the horse but gallop him on around after the field. I knew I had no chance, so why punish him. Suddenly at the three-eighths pole he began to run. He simply ate up the ground and came flying on the outside, passing horse after horse. I was dumbfounded at the move he made. We were only beaten a head at the wire. It seemed impossible.*[39]

The winner of that race, Huon Kid, was a nice horse but certainly nothing special. Noor, on the other hand, impressed Longden as something very special indeed with his courage and late burst of speed. The jockey hastily canceled his scheduled flight home and stayed in Northern California so he could try to convince Howard and Parke that he was the best rider for Noor in the future.

It worked.

Parke honored a commitment to another jockey, Ralph Neves, when Noor started next, closing out the year with a fifth-place finish in the San Carlos Handicap. Longden then was installed as Noor's regular rider. It would prove to be an extraordinarily successful partnership.

"One of the luckiest days in my life was at Tanforan when I rode Noor but lost to Huon Kid in the Tanforan Handicap," Longden said. "I know then that I had the winner of the Hundred Grander."[40]

Jockey John Longden in 1962. *Courtesy of* Thoroughbred Times.

A Miracle Year

Getting the mount on Noor in the Tanforan Handicap and then for the horse's spectacular 1950 season was pure happenstance, a matter of being in the right place at the right time, but Longden's good fortune shouldn't have come as a surprise. Luck always seemed to follow the rider.

Born in England just after the turn of the century, Longden immigrated to Canada with his family in 1912, when the lad was just five years old. The plan was to join Longden's father, Herb Longden, who had gone ahead to find work digging coal in Alberta. Sounds simple, but the Longdens almost didn't make it.

The train to Southampton already was running late on the Longden family's departure day. Then, any lingering hope of getting on board before the ship sailed was dashed when John wandered off into the crowd of onlookers packing the dock. The lost child turned up after a quick search, but by then the gangplanks were up, and the huge ship had cast off. It was April 10, four days before the RMS *Titanic* would crash into an iceberg south of Newfoundland. Of the 2,223 people on board the *Titanic*, only 710 survived.[41]

Eight decades later, Longden claimed that he always had a guardian angel perched on his shoulder.

"There he is now," Longden told a reporter. "He's got wings, and he's wearing white silks. He looks just like me. Actually, he's taller than me."[42]

Longden's guardian angel must have been a racing fan.

Like his father, Longden worked in the mines, driving the mules that pulled the ore carts. He was just a kid, but even then he dreamed about riding in races.

"I'd been reading all the books I could find about racing and horses and jockeys, and it was strongly in my mind that someday I could be a jockey," Longden recalled years later. "I was the right size for it. Sure, it was a kid's dream then, but if you make up your mind about something, think about it long enough, become determined it will be a reality, then you've got a fighting chance it will happen."[43]

Longden realized his dream when he left the mines at age twenty.

He rode his first official winner in 1927, a $300 claimer at a track outside Salt Lake City; his last winner, San Juan Capistrano Handicap winner George Royal, came in 1966. During the nearly four decades in between, Longden rode an amazing 32,413 races, won with 6,032 of them (18.6 percent) and retired with more victories than any other rider. He rode 1943 Triple Crown winner Count Fleet, five times led all riders in either races won or money earned, joined the Hall of Fame in 1958

Leading riders Bill Shoemaker, John Longden and Eddie Arcaro at Santa Anita in 1958. *Courtesy of* Thoroughbred Times.

and collected a special Eclipse Award in 1994. Longden also trained a Kentucky Derby winner, Majestic Prince. He was one of several riders and horsemen who established the Jockeys' Guild, which worked toward better working conditions for riders.

Longden earned a nickname, "the Pumper," for the distinctive back-and-forth pumping motion with his arms and legs he used to get a horse out of the starting gate quicker than anyone else and for his skill in keeping a horse driving to the finish line. He became known as a rider who was best with a front-runner, but in reality he was just as good with a horse that liked to come from behind.

Burley and the Pumper were exactly what Noor needed.

3
GREAT EXPECTATIONS

The Peter Principle[44] emerged in the late 1960s as a quasi-serious explanation for the ultimate inefficiency of any business. The idea is a simple one: in a well-run organization, competent employees are rewarded with promotions up through the management hierarchy, gaining more responsibility and authority with each step up. Problems ultimately arise when an employee moves into a job that he (or she) lacks the skills to perform, which will happen to almost everyone at some point as they move up the management ladder. Eventually, the theory goes, every position in the company will be filled by someone who is incompetent to perform the tasks at hand.

Thoroughbred racing has its own version of the Peter Principle. It's called the handicap division, and it works more or less the same way. The better a horse is, the more weight he will be asked to carry in a handicap race. Win under the weight assigned by the racing secretary in one race and more weight will be added for the next one. So it goes, onward and upward, until the horse finally is asked to carry a weight that he cannot handle successfully.

In theory, at least, the idea behind assigning weights to the horses in a handicap race is to level the playing field so that every horse in the field has at least a decent shot at winning. In practice, good horses are penalized for their success or at times for their reputations.[45]

Imagine telling New York Yankees manager Casey Stengel to bench Hall of Fame players Mickey Mantle and Yogi Berra in the fifth game of the 1953 World Series to give the Brooklyn Dodgers a better chance to win the game. That's how a handicap race works. This would never really happen in baseball, but it's a scenario that racing secretaries struggle with every day.

Shrewd weight assignments help fill races in the handicap division by giving lesser runners a fighting chance against better horses. Otherwise, owners might be tempted to skip the race and look for easier spots for their second-tier runners. The daunting task for the racing secretary is to come up with a weight spread between the stars and every other horse in the field that is wide enough to make the race interesting—but not too wide. It's a difficult balancing act. Sometimes racing secretaries get it right; sometimes they get it wrong and expect too much of even a great horse. It's a dilemma that gives rise to the old backstretch adage that "weight can stop a freight train."

Some "freight trains" are harder to stop than others. Horses that can handle high weights are rare—and legendary. Exterminator, which won one race under 138 pounds and nineteen others carrying 130 to 137 pounds, is one example; Discovery, which won eleven of nineteen races as a four-year-old carrying an average of 130 pounds, is another.[46]

Sitting at his desk in mid-December 1949, contemplating the $100,000-added Santa Anita Handicap two months hence, racing secretary Webb Everett faced a vexing question with no good answer: how much weight to put on Citation for the Big 'Cap. On paper, Citation was by far the strongest of the ninety-one nominees for the race, and the horse was the logical top weight.

But that was on paper. Look beyond his past performances, and Citation was as much of a question mark as a Triple Crown winner and Horse of the Year ever could be. The Calumet Farm star was sitting on a fifteen-race winning streak, but he had not gone to the track in earnest in more than a year, not since winning the Tanforan Handicap. His workouts had been good, but a workout is far from a race.

Complicating matters further was the timing.

Racing secretaries usually have the luxury of assigning weights much closer to a race than the two months Everett had to deal with, but he later defended the long lead time. Advance notice would give East Coast trainers sufficient time to ship to Santa Anita if they liked the weights, he explained, or to stay home if they didn't. Having the weights set two months before the Big 'Cap also would give trainers some flexibility in choosing prep races without the nagging worry that a good performance would boost the horses' imposts.[47]

Triple Crown–winner Citation on the track at Santa Anita. *Courtesy of Bill Mochon Archival Photo.*

Everett needed to make the Santa Anita Handicap competitive so it would fill and also so bettors would get their money's worth at the windows. At the same time, he didn't want to saddle Citation with so much weight that Jimmy Jones would balk and keep the horse in the barn. The Calumet star was the biggest draw for race fans, and a Santa Anita Handicap without Citation would be a public relations disaster for the track.

Everett realized that having a Big 'Cap without Citation was more than an idle threat. The possibility had to be seriously considered because Calumet had a strong bench and easily could win the race without Citation. In addition to Citation, Jones had 1949 Kentucky Derby winner Ponder and filly champion Two Lea to take up the slack. If the trainer entered all three horses, it would be the strongest entry ever for the Santa Anita Handicap and maybe the strongest entry anywhere. A one-two-three sweep for Calumet Farm wouldn't have surprised very many people.

The hole card for Everett, the lure for Calumet to run Citation no matter what the weights, was the huge purse for the Santa Anita Handicap—$100,000 added, with $97,000 net to the winner. A win would move Citation past Stymie as the leading money-winning Thoroughbred of all time and make the million-dollar mark tantalizingly close.

Charles S. Howard, who also had a horse entered in the Big 'Cap, understood the motivation, and he was intimately familiar with comebacks.

Seabiscuit, Horse of the Year in 1938, suffered a torn suspensory ligament, a serious injury that often ends a horse's career, in a prep race for the 1939 Santa Anita Handicap. Seabiscuit recuperated for a year at Howard's Ridgewood Ranch in Mendocino County, north of San Francisco, with breedings to seven mares a part of his rest and relaxation. The owner then surprised everyone by bringing the horse back to the races in 1940 to chase the career earnings record held at the time by Sun Beau.

Ironically, Seabiscuit passed Sun Beau and became the first Thoroughbred to earn more than $400,000 when he won the 1940 Santa Anita Handicap, Howard's goal in that year's race similar to Calumet's objectives with Citation a decade later. It was widely hailed as the greatest comeback in racing history, until Citation came along. The Triple Crown winner hadn't raced for a year in mid-December, but for Citation, the consensus question was *when* the comeback would be realized, not *if* there would be a comeback at all.

Everett finally settled on 132 pounds for Citation, 124 for Ponder and 113 for Two Lea. A controversial decision, it was more weight than Citation ever had been asked to carry. Nor had any previous winner of the Santa Anita Handicap won under such a high impost.

The high weight didn't scare off many bettors, though. Citation's odds to win in future book wagering at Agua Caliente racetrack in Mexico started short when the weights came out and only got shorter. By mid-January, the future book stopped taking bets on Citation to show and or finish fourth.

Noor, an Irish-bred five-year-old, was one of the lightweights on Everett's list. Noor was a nice horse with a wonderful pedigree and some promise, but he hadn't shown anything special, not yet. Third in the 1948 Epsom Derby for his breeder, the Aga Khan, and then purchased later the same year by Charles Howard, Noor did not make his first start in the United States until October 1949. Ironically, Noor was sidelined for several months with osselets after he arrived in the United States; it was the same injury that had kept Citation away from the races for a year.

Noor didn't give Everett a lot to work with. The horse won an allowance race in October 1949 at Bay Meadows, his first time out in Howard's red and white colors, and then placed in two of his next three races. In Noor's last start before Everett's weights for the Big 'Cap were released on December 14, he finished third, carrying 115 pounds, in the Tanforan Handicap on December 3.

The Tanforan performance didn't impress Everett all that much, and he assigned Noor 109 pounds, 23 pounds less than Citation. Noor ran twice more in 1949, finishing second in the San Francisco Handicap under 115 pounds and fifth in the San Carlos Handicap carrying 109 pounds, the same weight as his Santa Anita Handicap impost.

Robert Hebert, who covered California racing for the *Blood-Horse* magazine for decades, said that either Citation or Noor was being judged by a different, and inappropriate, standard.

"At 132 pounds, Citation had been handicapped off his 1948 form," Hebert said in his year-end wrap up.

> *That was fair enough. But at 109, *Noor was handicapped off his 1949 form, which consisted of three races that were merely tighteners, a third in the Tanforan Handicap and then an excellent second in the San Francisco Handicap. In that race he was left at the post, was beaten only a head at the wire by Huon Kid, and was probably 15 lengths the best. His 1949 form was something that should have been disregarded completely. Handicapped off his 1948 form (when the horse won two stakes and ran third in the Epsom Derby), as Citation was, *Noor would have been pegged at 120*

pounds or over. Any time a man pays as much for a horse as Owner C.S. Howard paid for *Noor, he must be able to run a little.[48]

Citation's 132-pound impost was worrisome, but there was no doubt at all about the strength of the Calumet entry for the Santa Anita Handicap. The main topic of conversation on the backstretch in the weeks leading up to the race had nothing to do with whether a Calumet horse would win; for most everyone, that was a given. The only real debate asked which of the three Calumet horses it would be.

The press generally conceded the Santa Anita Handicap to Citation, despite the 132 pounds he would be asked to carry. Or if not the 1948 Triple Crown winner and Horse of the Year, then 1949 Derby winner Ponder. Or maybe the filly champion Two Lea, which was getting a good break in the weights. Noor was given a chance by the supposed experts, but only a slight one, mainly because of the 23 pounds he would be getting from Citation.

"A handicap is supposed to bring the horses together and that's what I try to do," Everett said of his Big 'Cap weights.[49] With that objective in mind, 132 pounds for Citation and 109 pounds for Noor seemed reasonable at the time.

A lot can happen in two months, though—and a lot did.

More than two centuries ago, without a nod to the travails facing generations of racing secretaries to come, Scottish poet Robert Burns noted:

But, Mousie, thou art no thy lane
In proving foresight may be vain:
The best laid schemes o' mice an' men
Gang aft a-gley,
An' leav'e us nought but grief an' pain,
For promised joy.[50]

Webb Everett's best-laid schemes for the Santa Anita Handicap began to unravel during the first weeks of 1950, when topweight Citation proved vulnerable and Noor began to show signs of his true ability. Everett's Big

A Miracle Year

Noor working out with John Longden in the saddle. *Courtesy of Betfair Hollywood Park.*

'Cap weights were based on the anticipation that neither of those things would happen.

Jimmy Jones worked Citation between races on January 7 so the horse could hear the cheering crowd and get "racing minded after such a long layoff."[51] Four days later, Citation raced for the first time in thirteen months, extending his streak of consecutive victories to sixteen in a six-furlong allowance race. He carried 124 pounds, 8 less than his Santa Anita Handicap assignment, and he won by one and a half lengths.

Jones had not planned to run Citation if the track came up sloppy, which it did, but he decided at the last minute that the horse needed a race. Jones was satisfied with the result, but the stress of chasing Stymie's record and a million dollars was beginning to show on the trainer.

Jones admitted that training Citation had become a full-time job, and a difficult one.

"He is a twenty-four-hour worry to me," the Calumet trainer said. "I used to like to go to fights, football games, baseball games, ice hockey games and movies. But now I never get to see anything. Citation keeps my mind occupied the entire day and night. I say to myself, 'Have I done everything for the horse that it is possible for me to do?' And then I think of something that I did not do and I rush back to the barn."[52]

Despite the trainer's constant worry and attention, Citation's winning streak was snapped two weeks later in another allowance sprint.

Carrying 130 pounds for the first time in his career, Citation couldn't catch Miche in the stretch and lost by a neck. The race was six furlongs, Citation was giving Miche 16 pounds and Everett's 132-pound assignment for the Santa Anita Handicap was beginning to appear overly optimistic.

Noor, on the other hand, was starting to look like a good bet for the Big 'Cap at 109 pounds.

With just a week's rest after Noor's fifth-place finish in the San Carlos Handicap on New Year's Eve, trainer Burley Parke sent the Howard runner out for the San Pasqual Handicap at one and one-sixteenth miles. Noor was assigned 110 pounds for the San Pasqual, but veteran jockey John Longden couldn't make the weight, and the horse actually carried 112 pounds in the race. He was caught in a serious traffic jam on the first turn, ran wide coming into the stretch and then made a strong run through the stretch. Noor couldn't catch front-runner Solidarity, the winner by a length, but he finished a game second, three lengths clear of Calumet's Ponder. Noor was getting 9 pounds from the winner and 13 pounds from Ponder.

The San Pasqual was a reunion of sorts for Noor's owner, Charles S. Howard, and trainer Tom Smith, the genius behind Seabiscuit. Howard and Smith parted ways on friendly terms in 1943, three years after Seabiscuit's retirement, when Smith submitted to back surgery and was laid up for a year. Smith wound up training for Elizabeth Arden Graham, a cosmetics millionaire and owner of Maine Chance Farm. The Maine Chance entry for the San Pasqual, longshot The Poet, was close to the lead for a quarter mile but faded badly and finished twelfth in the fourteen-horse field.

Citation and Noor met for the first time on February 11, in the San Antonio Handicap at one and one-eighth miles. The San Antonio was the last serious prep race for horses being pointed toward the Santa Anita Handicap two weeks later, and it presented Webb Everett with another dilemma. His weights for the Big 'Cap, set in December and based mainly on his best guesses about the horses that would actually run, were carved in stone and couldn't be changed. Now, though, Everett had to assign weights for the San Antonio based on more timely information.

Citation had lost to lightweight Miche, Ponder had won the Santa Anita Maturity and Noor was looking a lot better than he had a month earlier. Some adjustments in the weights for the San Antonio were called for, but shuffling things around too much would call the Santa Anita Handicap weights—and the racing secretary's judgment—into question.

For the San Antonio, Everett did this:

	SAN ANTONIO	SANTA ANITA	DIFFERENCE
CITATION	130	132	-2
PONDER	128	124	+4
NOOR	114	109	+5

The San Antonio weights didn't affect the assignments for the Santa Anita Handicap, but they did indicate that Citation might have dropped a bit in Everett's estimation and that Ponder and Noor had come up a notch or two. Citation and Noor both prepped for the San Antonio with excellent workouts, covering a mile in 1:37 flat. It was the fastest time at that distance during the Santa Anita meeting for any horse, whether in a workout or in a race.

Jones had been concerned about Citation's weight—that there was too much of it—after the horse's layoff.[53] The trainer worked the horse hard when Citation was placed back in serious training, and by early February, the Calumet star had dropped some excess flesh and appeared to be in fighting trim.[54]

Citation edged Noor by a half length in the San Antonio, despite a sixteen-pound disadvantage in the weights, but Ponder beat them both, finishing a length clear of his stablemate. Miche, which had delivered Citation's first defeat in seventeen starts a few weeks earlier, never was a factor in the San Antonio and finished seventh.

It was the last time Citation would finish in front of Noor.

Optimistic weather reports the day before the San Antonio turned out to be wrong, and the race was run over a track labeled as "good." Noor had competed on an off track only once before, and after the San Antonio, jockey John Longden suggested that his mount hadn't liked the feel of the racing strip very much. Noor's third-place finish didn't sway Longden's confidence, and he didn't waver in his earlier prediction that Noor still was the horse to beat in the Santa Anita Handicap.[55] Longden backed up his confidence with a $100 winter book bet on Noor to win.

Charles Howard was less certain.

Winning the Santa Anita Handicap had been one of Howard's principal goals from the race's inception in 1935, and his horses had compiled by a wide margin the best record for any owner. He already had a pair of Big 'Cap winners to his credit—Seabiscuit in 1940 and Kayak II the previous year—and narrow misses in three other runnings of the race. In one of Seabiscuit's losses, by a hard-fought nose to Stagehand in 1938,[56] the Howard runner carried thirty pounds more than the winner. Howard, as much as anyone, understood the difference weight can make.

By 1950, the owner's health was failing, and he desperately wanted another win in the Santa Anita Handicap. Despite a twenty-three-pound concession from Citation, Noor still seemed an unlikely candidate to take Howard to the winner's circle for a third time.

"If, and that's a great word around a racetrack, if Noor knew how to leave the gate and get a position like Seabiscuit, I'd say we had a chance," Howard said. "Now, I only say we have a hope. Noor just hasn't mastered the art of leaving the starting gate. Until he does, he'll have a tough time beating horses like Citation and Ponder."[57]

So far, Howard was correct. He didn't mention that Noor also was having a hard time handling good horses like Solidarity and a handful of lesser lights that kept beating the horse to the finish line. Noor was a closer with only one good stretch run. Commentary in his *Daily Racing Form* past performances suggested that the horse was either contending at the finish in the races he didn't win ("closed fast," "game effort," "gaining fast," "late rush") or had some sort of excuse ("raced wide" or "off slowly").

Added distance in the Santa Anita Handicap—at one and a quarter miles, a furlong longer than the San Antonio—might help compensate for Noor's persistent gate problems and his slow starts by giving John Longden a little more time to get the horse in gear; that is, if the Pumper was up to it.

4

The Big 'Cap

Three days before the Santa Anita Handicap, while the field was making its way to the starting gate for the last race on the afternoon's program, a horse named Alfa started acting up. The fractious animal tossed her rider, John Longden, who injured his left ankle and knee in the fall. Longden had lobbied hard with owner Charles Howard to get the mount on Noor, and now, seventy-two hours before the Santa Anita Handicap, he found himself limping back to the jocks' room, his status for the big race uncertain.

Charles Howard was famously loyal to people who worked for him, and he treated trainer Tom Smith and jockey Red Pollard more like family than employees. But that loyalty had its limits. Howard and Smith had not been reluctant to change riders for Seabiscuit when Red Pollard was injured; now it was up to Howard and Burley Parke to decide what to do about Longden. The Pumper was a good fit for Noor, but was a gimpy Longden good enough to go up against the likes of Citation and Ponder?

Riders can be a superstitious lot, and Longden surprisingly accepted the injury as a good omen. It brought back memories of another fall, followed by a win in an important race.

Longden was supposed to ride First Fiddle in the 1944 Butler Handicap in New York. The day before the Butler, Longden was riding a filly named Dine and Dance. She shied from a piece of paper blowing across the track and slammed into the rail, and Longden came off. Horses trailing Dine and Dance galloped over the fallen rider, and he wound up with a broken foot.

First Fiddle was one of the best horses Longden rode during the mid-1940s. The Butler was a rich race for the time, and he didn't want to lose the mount—or the jockey's 10 percent of the purse.

"I didn't want to let Eddie Mulrehan [who owned First Fiddle] down," Longden said, "so I had the doc shoot that busted foot so full of Novocain I couldn't feel a thing. I knew First Fiddle ran better for me than anyone else, and I felt I could win the race. Eddie needed the money—it was a big pot for those days, fifty thousand added."[58]

Longden finally consented to have a cast put on the broken foot—but only after First Fiddle crossed the finish line first in the Butler. Longden was bedridden the next day, but it was because of severe back pain, not the broken foot. The jockey, it turned out, won the Butler with a broken foot and two fractured vertebrae.[59]

No bones were broken when Alfa tossed Longden—maybe it was the rider's guardian angel at work again—but Longden's foot was so swollen and painful the next day that the jockey couldn't put on a shoe. Longden took himself off all his mounts for Thursday and Friday so he could stay home and treat the injury with hot compresses, but he reported that he would be ready to ride Noor in the Santa Anita Handicap on the weekend.

Howard and Parke took the veteran rider at his word.

Over on the Calumet side, the pre-race omens were more problematic.

The day before Longden came off Alfa, Steve Brooks had been thrown by a maiden filly named Acquiescence. She bolted at the start and crashed through a temporary rail, and Brooks hit the ground hard. He somersaulted twice, got to his feet and walked away from the crash. It was a close call for the Calumet Farm contract rider, who was scheduled to ride Ponder in the Big 'Cap. Unlike Longden, Brooks looked none the worse for wear after the accident.[60]

Calumet trainer Jimmy Jones wasn't so lucky. The day before the Santa Anita Handicap, someone broke into Jones's apartment near the track and carried off everything of value—cash, clothes, jewelry and even a small portable radio where the trainer had tucked away eight $100 bills for safe keeping.

Jones always was a sharp dresser, and the loss of his wardrobe must have hurt. Of the sixty-five thousand or so people who showed up for the thirteenth Santa Anita Handicap, he probably was the only one at the track wearing a borrowed suit.[61]

A Miracle Year

Ninety-one horses were nominated for the 1950 Santa Anita Handicap, eleven were entered and that many answered the call to the post on February 25. Citation was the top weight, with 132 pounds. Closest to him in the weights was stablemate Ponder, with 124 pounds, and My Request, with 122. There were few surprises when Jimmy Jones named the riders for the Calumet entry—Eddie Arcaro on Citation; Steve Brooks on Ponder; Johnny Gilbert on Two Lea—although Brooks had won the Santa Margarita Handicap with Two Lea and would have been a logical choice to ride the filly.

Citation coming onto the track for the Santa Anita Handicap. *Courtesy of Bill Mochon Archival Photo.*

Calumet was the perennial leader among stables, and the Calumet horses attracted some of the best jockeys in the land, both contract and freelance. The Santa Anita Handicap was no exception.

Eddie Arcaro won Triple Crowns for Calumet with Whirlaway and Citation,[62] and he was in the midst of a Hall of Fame career. He would retire in 1961 with five Kentucky Derbies, six Preakness Stakes, six Belmont Stakes, ten Jockey Club Gold Cups, eight Suburban Handicaps and four Metropolitan Handicaps to his credit. He was the leading money winner among jockeys six times, and his horses earned more than $30 million.

Steve Brooks, another jockey destined for the Hall of Fame, was riding a hot streak—he had been the country's leading jockey in both races won and purse money earned in 1949. The relative lack of attention accorded Johnny Gilbert, winner of a national riding title himself, was a testament to the talents of Arcaro and Brooks.

With Stymie's career earnings record in sight for Citation, speculation was rampant on the backstretch and in the press that Jimmy Jones would instruct Brooks and Gilbert to hold their horses back if that's what it took for the Calumet star to win the Santa Anita Handicap. Jones never officially "declared" Calumet's intention to win with Citation rather than with Ponder or Two Lea, but a pre-race announcement that the three Calumet riders would divide their winnings equally lent some credence to the rumors.[63] An even split of the winnings might make instructions to let Citation win more palatable to the losing riders.

Similar speculation surrounded the 1940 Santa Anita Handicap, when Charles Howard's entry of Seabiscuit and Kayak II ran one-two as the odds-on favorite. The winner's share of the purse made Seabiscuit the world's richest Thoroughbred, eclipsing the old record held by Sun Beau. The career earnings mark had been one of Howard's long-standing goals for Seabiscuit, and the Big 'Cap was the horse's best—and as things turned out, his last—opportunity to establish a new record. Many observers thought that Kayak II ran a stronger race than his stablemate and that jockey Buddy Haas held the horse back at the finish, giving Seabiscuit the victory.[64]

Whether Citation could win on his own merits, or if necessary with some help from the riders on Ponder and Two Lea, was a relevant question only if the Calumet trio was together at the finish. The strategy would be meaningless if Webb Everett's weights for the race brought the field together as he hoped, making every horse a legitimate threat.

Noor got in the race with a 109-pound assignment, the lightest of the eleven starters, and that presented a problem for the Irish import's rider.

John Longden was small, even for a jockey, standing four feet, eleven inches and weighing in the neighborhood of 109 pounds. He probably could make the weight assigned to Noor if he rode naked and without tack, but clothed in a helmet, silks, jockey pants and boots, and carrying a lightweight racing saddle, Longden's usual working weight was around 114 pounds. Going up in weight for a race was a simple matter of adding some lead pads to the saddle; reducing when there is precious little weight to lose, on the other hand, was a more difficult proposition.

Longden promised Howard and Parke that come hell or high water he could make the weight assigned to Noor, or at least come close to it—and he did, dieting and sweating for weeks until he tipped the scales at 110 pounds on Big 'Cap day.

The tote board in the Santa Anita infield showed the total money bet to win, place and show on each horse in each race.[65] Because Citation, Ponder and Two Lea all were owned by Calumet Farm, they were coupled as a single entry for wagering purposes. A bet on one horse in the Devil's Red silks was a bet on all three. It was inconceivable that all three Calumet horses would finish out of the money, and bets on the entry to show went through the roof. There was so much show money coming through the betting windows, in fact, that the tote board couldn't handle it all.

No bettor would get rich betting the Calumet entry to show. The smallest payout on a winning ticket allowed by law was five cents on the dollar, $2.10 for a $2.00 ticket and so on, but it was a 5 percent return on an investment with what amounted to an iron-clad guarantee.

Ten minutes after betting opened, show money wagered on the Calumet entry topped the $100,000 mark, and members of the Santa Anita electrical crew had to tack up a small board with a numeral "1" painted on it. The tote board wasn't designed with a Citation/Ponder/Two Lea entry in mind and indicated only five-figure totals. A painted "2" went up a few minutes later, followed by a "3." Betting closed before it became necessary to amend the total a fourth time.

Of the $1,009,846 bet on the Santa Anita Handicap, more than one-third ($373,268) was bet on the Calumet entry to show.

Noor was the only other horse in the field that attracted any significant money from bettors, starting as second choice at odds of more than six to one. Odds on the others ranged from eleven to one on My Request to fifty-two to one on But Why Not.

If there was supposed to be some sort of gentleman's agreement among the Calumet riders to give Eddie Arcaro and Citation the right of way if they needed it to win the Santa Anita Handicap, jockey Johnny Gilbert apparently didn't get the message.

Calumet had so many good horses waiting in the wings that trainer Jimmy Jones had the luxury of using a champion—the filly Two Lea—as a rabbit in the Santa Anita Handicap, and Gilbert set a blistering pace with her from the start. After a mile in $1:35^{1}/_{5}$, faster than the track record for the distance, Two Lea still was in front and hugging the rail.

John Longden had Noor in second on the outside thanks to an early move on the backstretch that no one expected. Ponder was coming up from next-to-last, and Longden sent Noor with him. For a horse better known as a one-run closer, it was a gutsy move.

"Use your own judgment," was all Parke had said to his rider in the paddock before the race, and the trainer was surprised when Longden's judgment had Noor a length off Two Lea after six furlongs.

"Some may have criticized Longden for moving as early as he did nearing the five-and-one-half-furlong pole," Parke said after the race, "but if he hadn't done so, Ponder was going to hem him in as he did in the San Antonio Handicap. Longden got him out of that impending jam in a hurry and still had plenty of run left in his horse when he made his vital move around the far turn."[66] Unsaid but understood: It was a smart move by John Longden only because it paid off and Noor ultimately won. If Noor had come up short in the stretch after moving earlier than usual, it would have been a much different story.

Citation, meanwhile, had escaped some serious interference earlier in the race and was in contention, but he needed some help.

A Miracle Year

Going into the first turn, Citation was racing shoulder to shoulder with Old Rockport on the rail to his left and My Request to his right when My Request suddenly veered in sharply. With nowhere to go, Arcaro eased Citation back out of trouble. Seconds later, Solidarity slammed into My Request, shoving him into Old Rockport. The riding infractions were serious enough that Eric Guerin, the jockey on My Request, and Ralph Neves, on Solidarity, were suspended for the rest of the Santa Anita meeting.

Citation was running third when the leaders turned into the stretch, behind Two Lea on the rail and Noor to his outside. Eddie Arcaro shouted for Gilbert to move Two Lea off the rail and give him some room to run, but the filly didn't budge. Either Gilbert didn't hear Arcaro or he thought he could win the race himself.

"We had Two Lea out there to set the pace for him," Jones recalled, "and Arcaro figured for sure Johnny Gilbert would move the filly out a little bit and let him through, but Gilbert stayed right on the rail, and Arcaro had to take up and go around her, so he lost momentum there.

"And there was where Noor just rushed by him. At the eighth pole, Two Lea still had the lead by a head, but Noor was taking her, and Citation was two lengths back and getting a little rubbery; but he came on again, and got beat only 1¼ lengths, giving him 22 pounds and him breaking the track record."[67]

Noor covered the one and a quarter miles in two minutes, breaking the old track mark by one and one-fifth seconds. The previous record had stood for a decade, since Seabiscuit won the 1940 Santa Anita Handicap.

Noor defeats Citation in the Santa Anita Handicap. Courtesy of Thoroughbred Times.

A charging Citation finished a game second, a length in front of Two Lea. Ponder was fourth, a neck farther back. The Calumet entry that was expected to finish one-two-three instead ran two-three-four. It was a crushing blow for the Calumet faithful.

By the time Noor and Longden made it back to the winner's circle, where Charles and Marcella Howard, Burley Parke, Longden's wife Hazel and a blanket of carnations were waiting, the Pumper looked like he was about to keel over. Reducing to make the weight, stress from the painful leg injury he had suffered when he was thrown a few days earlier and a hard-fought victory on a horse that was difficult to handle all had taken their toll. Reporters who said that Longden looked "a little pale"[68] were being kind.

"I damn near fainted in the winner's circle after the race," Longden recalled.[69] He needed help dismounting from Noor, and making his way to the scales to weigh in was a struggle for the little man.

Years later, before the 1959 running of the Santa Anita Handicap, Longden said the victory with Noor was his greatest thrill among his victories in the race—and the most difficult.

"I had to do awful light on him," Longden told television reporter Gil Stratton in the Santa Anita paddock. "I took off four pounds that morning. I guess I took off too much, although it paid off."[70]

Charles Howard was ecstatic about his new star Thoroughbred.

"That was a thrill, a great one," he said. "You know, I haven't been to the winner's circle lately. It was a pleasure."

Someone asked if Noor was another Seabiscuit, and Howard, smiling, shook his head.

"Not in my affections yet. But he'll do, he'll do."[71]

Howard ordered champagne for the press box after the race, a gesture reporters had missed since the heyday of Seabiscuit, and he spent the rest of the afternoon chatting with well-wishers about Noor's victory.

The Santa Anita Handicap was the first of four epic battles between Noor and Citation in 1950, but it turned out to be the only one of the four that Charles Howard would be able to see in person. Stricken with heart problems and unable to withstand the excitement of watching his horses compete, he was too ill to watch the San Juan Capistrano Handicap just a week later. Howard died of a heart attack on June 6, days before Noor and Citation turned in a pair of stunning, world-record performances at Golden Gate Fields in Northern California.

Racing historian William H.P. Robertson, for years the editor of the *Thoroughbred Record* (now the *Thoroughbred Times*), later called the Noor-

Burley Parke and John Longden joined Charles and Marcella Howard in the winner's circle after the Santa Anita Handicap. *Courtesy of Bill Mochon Archival Photo.*

Citation races "the most enigmatic sequence of handicap races in American turf annals."[72]

For racing fans in California, the fun had just begun.

5

"Greatest Race I've Ever Seen!"[73]

A popular pastime in the days following the Santa Anita Handicap was speculating about excuses for Citation's loss to Noor, and there were plenty to choose from: Citation in 1950 still was a good horse, but he had lost a step or two since his Triple Crown season; Citation was sore; Citation needed more time to train and came up short for the Big 'Cap; the obvious interference inflicted by My Request early in the race; Johnny Gilbert's inexplicable failure to move Two Lea out and give Eddie Arcaro and Citation the rail; and the weights—always the weights.

Webb Everett defended his assessments of the Santa Anita Handicap field after Noor's unexpected win.

"All second guessers look good after the race is won," the veteran racing secretary and handicapper said.

> *Before the handicap, as I recall, virtually every expert around here seemed to think the weights were OK.* [Jimmy Jones didn't like the weights, but he had a vested interest.] *At least the great majority picked Citation, Ponder, and Two Lea ahead of Noor.*
>
> *After they looked at the pictures which showed that Citation was jammed at the first turn it seemed to be the consensus that he still would have won if he didn't have trouble.*
>
> *We had to make those weights on Dec. 14 before any of the horses had run here but, frankly, I wouldn't have changed my handicap more than two or three pounds if I made it after the race was run.*[74]

There even was some second-guessing about the decision to run Citation in the race at all.

Twenty-five years later, discussing Citation's loss to Noor in the Santa Anita Handicap with veteran turf writer Joe Hirsch, Jimmy Jones said that Citation needed more time to be ready for the race. Jones admitted that in retrospect he regretted acceding to Calumet owner Warren Wright's wishes about running Citation:

> *Perhaps if I had been head trainer for Calumet 10 years or so at the time, or if I'd been a little older, I would have told Mr. Wright that I wasn't quite ready with Citation, and he wouldn't run in the big race. However, I had the feeling that I was sent to California to do a job, and that was to win the Santa Anita Handicap.*[75]

Despite the bitter disappointment, Jones was magnanimous in public.

"As long as we had to get beaten," he told reporters after the Santa Anita Handicap, "I certainly was glad to have a horse owned by C.S. Howard do it. He is one of California's grand sportsmen and he has done a lot for the racing game."[76]

Inside, though, the Calumet trainer was seething about a loss he felt came about more through "the strike of a pen"[77] than because Noor was the better horse. It was an obvious reference to the 132 pounds put on Citation by Webb Everett. Jones continued to rail against the unfairness of handicap racing in general and the imposts assigned Citation in particular.

"I'll tell you just how bad I feel about it," Jones said a few days after the Santa Anita Handicap,

> *it makes me want to quit the game. I'm not talking about the money at all. It would have been nice to get that far nearer his goal and all that, but I'm not worried about the money. You get to think of a horse like Citation as if he was a relative or a close friend, and seeing him beaten takes the heart out of you.*
>
> *He ran one of his top races in the Santa Anita...Had he won, it would have been the crowning achievement of my career with the horse and, to me, his defeat by the lightweight of the field—but a horse who was, nevertheless, good enough to finish third in the Epsom Derby—bears out all the arguments I have ever used against our system of handicaps.*
>
> *I will tell you one thing. Citation—yes, and any horse—only has a limited number of such races to offer. Say four or five at the most. The*

> strain is too great. It is hard enough on legs and tendons and muscles, but a great horse is more than his physical make-up. What makes a great horse is that indefinable something inside him, and I ask you—how many times, giving his all under top weights, conceding over 20 pounds to other good thoroughbreds, can he have dust thrown in his face? It does something to them, that's all.[78]

There were nuggets of truth in all of the excuses raised in defense of Citation, and some of them were still being raised decades later. The excuses all failed to take into account one very important fact, however. Under Burley Parke's skilled and patient tutelage and Longden's inspired riding, Noor was developing into a very good horse, almost certainly the best handicapper on the West Coast and maybe the best handicapper anywhere. To prove to the doubters that his win in the Santa Anita Handicap was not a fluke—and the doubters were legion, even after the Santa Anita Handicap—Noor would have to beat Citation again, maybe over and over again. And the weights the two horses carried would have to be closer.

Noor's next chance was seven days away, in the San Juan Capistrano Handicap, if Citation showed up.

Jones really wanted Citation and Noor to meet at level weights, but there were few weight-for-age opportunities for older horses in major races. He was coy about whether Citation would start in the days leading up to the San Juan Capistrano, probably a half-hearted attempt to influence Everett's deliberations about the weights.

"It is too soon to say definitely, one way or the other," Jones said the day after the Santa Anita Handicap.

> He cooled out fine and he's in good shape this morning...but I want to wait a couple of days at least to judge what the effects of a long race as severe as the Santa Anita may have been. As I said before, great horse as he is—and I never expect to see another one like him—he has not got too many of that kind of races left, and I must deal the remaining ones out carefully.
>
>   Then, too, the weights for Saturday's race will have a bearing on the decision.[79]

If Citation was sound, and there was no reason to think otherwise, there was little doubt that he would run in the San Juan Capistrano. In light of Warren Wright's dogged determination that Citation be racing's first million-dollar earner, what Jones's waffling really meant was that Citation would run unless the horse had to carry Webb Everett himself.

Money, in the form of Stymie's earnings mark and the million-dollar plateau, was on everyone's mind. Citation picked up $20,000 with his second-place finish in the Santa Anita Handicap, bringing Stymie's record that much closer. A win in the $50,000-added San Juan Capistrano would move Citation into first place among the world's richest Thoroughbreds, bringing one of Warren Wright's goals for the horse to fruition.

Maybe more importantly, Jones wanted to put to rest the first hints of speculation that Noor and Citation were in the same league.

"I wanted to vindicate Citation," Jones told Joe Hirsch. "He had lost a race I felt he could and should have won. So I entered him in the San Juan Capistrano Handicap at a mile and three-quarters just one week later."[80]

Citation got a break of sorts when Webb Everett assigned weights for the San Juan Capistrano, scheduled as the feature race on closing day at Santa Anita.

Everett had Citation and Ponder as the co-topweights with 130 pounds each, 2 pounds less than Citation had carried in the Santa Anita Handicap against a 6-pound increase for Ponder. Noor picked up the most weight, 8 pounds from Everett's Big 'Cap assessment, 7 pounds more than the weight he actually carried in the race. Barring another accident, Longden would be sound for the San Juan Capistrano, and he would have no problem at all with the horse's 117-pound impost.

Webb Everett's assessment of the San Juan Capistrano Handicap was concise and straight to the point: "Greatest race I've ever seen!"[81]

A bit of prejudice on Everett's part would have been understandable, since he authored a racing secretary's dream finish in the San Juan Capistrano, but hardly anyone among the sixty thousand racing fans who turned out on getaway day would argue with him.

With five furlongs to go, first Citation and then Noor began to draw away from the other six starters. For the last half mile, the San Juan Capistrano became the match race everyone wanted to see: Citation's supporters seeking vindication for the horse's loss in the Santa Anita Handicap and

Noor (#3) edges Citation by a nose in the San Juan Capistrano Handicap. *Courtesy of Thoroughbred Times.*

Noor's followers hoping for confirmation that their horse really could run with anyone.

Robert Hebert, longtime California correspondent for the *Blood-Horse* magazine, described the finish this way:

> **Noor has to be a good horse to do the things he did in the San Juan Capistrano Handicap. Both on his part, and on Citation's, it was a much better performance than either showed in the Santa Anita handicap. This time Racing Secretary Webb Everett had the weights just about right, 130 pounds for Citation and 117 for *Noor, and it turned out to be the greatest race ever run at Santa Anita. It was very easily the greatest race this reporter has ever seen, or expects to see, and it will, very probably, go down in the tomes as one of the classics of the American Turf.*
>
> *Every step of the last five-sixteenths of a mile, Citation and Noor were together, stride for stride. At the quarter pole, Noor, on the outside, had an advantage of perhaps a head. In mid-stretch, Citation had battled his way to the top by a quarter of a length. Ten yards from the wire,*

Citation still looked like the winner; then Noor, calling on some untapped reserve of speed and courage under an inspired ride by Longden, came along to arch his head under the wire in what must surely have been the last jump. Both horses were straight as a string at the finish. The camera caught them both with heads outstretched, as they were reaching for that elusive finish line. The margin was a couple of inches, and it belonged to Noor.[82]

Noor and Citation already were pulling up when Mocopo crossed the finish line in third place, almost thirteen lengths behind the winner.

Years later, Jimmy Jones echoed Webb Everett, calling the San Juan Capistrano the best race he ever saw:

The greatest race I ever saw was the race between Citation and Noor (San Juan Capistrano Handicap, 1¾ miles, March 4, 1950). Noor was a young horse, his whole life in front of him, sound, had 117 on him. Citation had 130. I swear...the valets were sitting down there at the winner's circle...right on the finish line. These were old time jocks that had seen a lot of races. And they all said, "Well, you won." I said, "I don't know; it was awful close." Well they gave it to Noor, by the closest of noses. But you know I never did see the photo finish picture. I turned around and saw Citation coming back to me, takin' short steps. The ol' ankle had given away again. I assume it gave away in that drive. They were, it seemed to me, a sixteenth of a mile in front of the field. It's the only time I left the track feelin' bad. My horse broke down, but I got him patched up and ran him in San Francisco and he broke the world's record, but it was a patch job.[83]

Veteran Santa Anita announcer Joe Hernandez concurred. Of the twenty-five thousand or so races he called during his career, Hernandez said that the 1950 San Juan Capistrano was "the most exciting race," one that left him "limp."[84]

Noor now had the distinction of being the only horse ever to defeat Citation twice. He still was getting weight from the Calumet star, but the differential in the San Juan Capistrano was not as much as the spread that had separated the two horses in the Santa Anita Handicap (twenty-two pounds then, thirteen pounds now). If any doubts about Noor's class as a racehorse lingered after the rousing photo finish, they quickly were dispelled by a glance at the electronic timer. Noor had covered the one and three-quarters miles in a blistering 2:52$^{4/5}$, a clocking that lowered the previous American record (2:54$^{3/5}$) by almost two full seconds.

For a time, there was some dispute about the status of Noor's clocking as a new world record. Almost thirty years earlier, in the Gran Premio Jose Ramirez, run at a track in Montevideo, Uruguay, Buen Ojo had been timed at 2:52$^{3/5}$ for a similar distance. Similar is not the same as equal, however, and some mathematically inclined racing fans with a lot of free time on their hands pointed out that the distance for Buen Ojo's record-setting race had been measured in meters. After some calculations, it turned out that Buen Ojo's record-setting race was run at 2,800 meters, which happens to be about fifty-three feet *shorter* than one and three-quarters miles. This meant that Noor had taken one-fifth of a second longer than Buen Ojo, but he also had covered more ground.

When the 1952 edition of the *American Racing Manual* was released, Noor's time for the San Juan Capistrano was officially recognized as a world record.[85] It would be the first of a string of record-setting performances for Noor.

Charles Howard was able to attend the first few races on closing day, but fear that the excitement of a close finish would overtax an ailing heart compelled him to leave before the San Juan Capistrano was run. Marcella Howard reported Noor's victory to her husband by telephone and accepted the gold trophy on his behalf.[86]

After the race, Longden said that the San Juan Capistrano was the "toughest race I've ever ridden."[87] He heaped praise on both Noor and Citation for their efforts:

"I have to take my hat off to Citation. He's truly great. Noor was headed in the drive to the wire, but I had a great horse under me and we had to go all out to beat a marvelous champion."[88]

Noor came out of the San Juan Capistrano sound and ready to race again. Citation did not.

"We lost more than the race that day," Jimmy Jones said. "Citation came back to me lame. I really felt awful about that. It was a distressing thing."[89]

Citation wouldn't race again for two and a half months.

A press box poll at Santa Anita tabbed Citation as the "best horse of the meeting" and the Santa Anita Handicap as the best race of the season. Noor was ranked third among handicap horses, trailing both Citation and Ponder. The only problem with the poll was that the voting took place *before* the San Juan Capistrano Handicap was run, rather than afterward, when Noor and the San Juan Capistrano almost certainly would have been ranked higher by the turf writers casting ballots.

Racing fans turn out to see Noor. *Courtesy of the Parke family.*

The results of the premature poll foreshadowed a more important championship vote later in the year when Noor again wouldn't receive full credit for his record because the results were tabulated before an important race.

California racing packed its bags and moved north to Tanforan Racetrack, near San Francisco, when the meeting at Santa Anita ended. The picturesque track had a checkered history.[90] In addition to horse racing, Tanforan at various times hosted dog races, motorcycle races and, around the turn of the century, bizarre contests pitting automobiles against airplanes. The track also served as a backdrop for *Riding High*, a Frank Capra motion picture that starred an up-and-comer named Bing Crosby.

Writing about the movie, which made it to the big screen during the 1950 Tanforan meeting, sportswriter Prescott Sullivan was optimistic about Crosby's chances to make it in show business.

"The fella has a good deal of ability," Prescott opined. "He sings, dances and acts, and it's hard to tell what he's best at. After you've seen him, we think you'll agree that he ought to go far."[91]

Prescott's tongue-in-cheek review was accurate but a little late—Crosby had been a box office draw for years—and it demonstrated one of the great truths of horse racing: it's easy to handicap a race after it's been run.

A Miracle Year

Tanforan served as a military training center during World War I and as an infamous internment camp for Japanese Americans detained during World War II on the orders of President Franklin Roosevelt.[92]

Legendary Australian champion Phar Lap spent time at Tanforan preparing for his race in the Agua Caliente Handicap in Mexico, and Seabiscuit raced there, winning the Marchbank Handicap in 1937. Both Noor and Citation also had historical ties to Tanforan. The track was where Noor first attracted the attention of John Longden with a fast-closing, second-place finish in the 1949 San Francisco Handicap. Citation had won the Tanforan Handicap a year earlier, in the horse's last race before injury forced him to the sidelines for the entire 1949 season.

Fervent hope among track management and racing fans alike was that Noor and Citation would renew their rivalry during the 1950 Tanforan meeting, possibly in a match race but more likely in the Tanforan Handicap. Either would be wildly popular and a financial windfall for the track, and a showdown between the two horses was heavily promoted.

Burley Parke shot down the idea of a match race a few days after the San Juan Capistrano, calling the idea "absurd." The problem, he said, was not so much the match race itself but the aftermath.

"If a match race could be arranged at equal weights, and my horse could win," Parke said, "he would have weight piled on him beyond normal racing conditions."[93]

The purse for the Tanforan Handicap was doubled, from $25,000 added to the $50,000 added, in an effort to entice the two horses to run, but that didn't work, either.

Calumet won the Tanforan Handicap, but with Ponder, not Citation.

Jimmy Jones skipped the entire Tanforan meeting with Citation, going on record to say that the Santa Anita and San Juan Capistrano Handicaps, two hard-fought races run just a week apart, required more recovery time than the Tanforan schedule allowed.

"Those two races took more out of my horse than was visible to the eye," Jones said.

> *I don't think any race at one mile and three-quarters is a fair test for Thoroughbreds.*
>
> *If the Tanforan Handicap was to be run on the closing day of the meeting, I think I could get my horse ready. But I just don't relish the thought of pounding it to him like I did at Santa Anita. Citation has been good to me, and I want to be good to him.*[94]

Not that it mattered a whit with Citation almost certainly a non-starter, but the horse was assigned top weight of 132 pounds for the Tanforan Handicap anyway. Ponder was next, with 129 pounds, followed by Noor (124) and Two Lea (118).

Even without the lure of a Citation-Noor matchup, the Tanforan Handicap still had the potential to be a marquee event. Northern California was Charles Howard's home turf, where he had a huge fan base; Noor was a rising star, and Ponder was, after all, a Kentucky Derby winner. The bottom fell out a few hours before post time, when Howard announced that Noor was hurt and would not run.

"It's a bitter blow," Howard said, "but in fairness to the public, and to the horse, he must be declared."[95]

Two days before the Tanforan Handicap, during a five-furlong workout, Noor had tried to jump over a shadow on the racetrack. He stumbled, almost fell and hit his left foreleg with a hind hoof. The injury didn't seem serious at the time, and Burley Parke didn't think the horse would be scratched.

"He's just a big, clumsy kid," Parke said while he watched Noor being cooled out after the workout. "He must've thought the shadow was a hole, and took off like a steeplechaser. All four feet were high off the ground and he seemed to be swimming. Thank goodness he came down straight. He's so full of the dickens now I get a slight case of heart failure every time he's out of his stall."[96]

There was swelling in Noor's injured leg on Friday morning, but by the end of the day the leg looked normal. Parke was hopeful that Noor could race the next day, but after a gallop early Saturday morning, there was heat and swelling in the leg again.

Veterinarian Roy E. Lovell examined the leg and gave a cautionary prognosis.

The stress of racing might result in a more serious injury, like a bowed tendon, Dr. Lovell said. "On the other hand," he added, "this horse could run to his best and not suffer any ill effects. If I owned Noor, I would not run him because he has too brilliant a future."[97]

Even though he thought Noor probably could run in the Tanforan Handicap, Burley Parke reluctantly agreed with the veterinarian's assessment.

"Do you think we should run Noor?" Howard asked the trainer.

"Mr. Howard, I do not own Noor," Parke replied.

"But just suppose that you did own Noor. Would you run him?"

"I sure would like to own a horse like Noor."

"Just for the purpose of gaining an answer," Howard pressed, "let's say that you own Noor. Now then, as his owner, would you run him?'

"As his owner, Mr. Howard," Parke finally said, "I definitely would not run Noor."[98]

Obviously disappointed, Howard finally acquiesced:

> *I dearly wanted to see Noor run against Ponder and against the other fine horses, but in fairness to the horse and to the public, I have no alternative but to scratch him.*
>
> *It is my opinion, and it is Burley Parke's opinion, that Noor right now is capable of running a fine race and giving Ponder a real argument, but I do sincerely think that the best interests of all will be served by not running him when my veterinarian advises against it.*[99]

The Howards were represented in the winner's circle after the Tanforan Handicap, but not in the way Charles Howard, Burley Park and John Longden anticipated. Marcella Howard presented the winner's trophy to Jimmy Jones after Ponder edged Old Rockport in near-track-record time.

The much-anticipated renewal between Noor and Citation would have to wait.

It was a rematch that Noor's owner never would see.

Charles S. Howard suffered a fatal heart attack on June 6 at his home in Hillsborough, a well-to-do suburb outside San Francisco. He always will be remembered best as the owner of Seabiscuit, the Depression-era horse that truly was an American legend, as author Laura Hillenbrand famously proclaimed in her bestseller, *Seabiscuit*. But Howard did as much as anyone of his time to erase the long-standing prejudice against California racing harbored by many East Coast horsemen.

Years before California-bred Swaps shipped east under the radar to upset Horse of the Year Nashua in the 1955 Kentucky Derby, Howard took on all comers. Seabiscuit was Kentucky-bred, and Noor was an import from Ireland, but both horses were Californians through and through. They were adopted and embraced by their fans and, like Howard himself, were wildly popular in the Golden State.

Seabiscuit crisscrossed the country by train during the 1930s, chalking up thousands of miles and holding his own against the best horses the East Coast establishment could muster against him. Then Noor defeated Citation, and Ponder, and Two Lea, and Triple Crown–winner Assault and Horse of the Year Hill Prince, all on his home turf, usually setting world records in the process. California races, it turned out, weren't always the lucrative soft spots they were supposed to be. Thanks to Howard, West Coast racing was starting to lose its status as an ugly stepchild.

The majority of Howard's horses had been sold by the end of the year, a few privately but most in a 108-horse dispersal at Santa Anita that grossed $227,400. Nathoo was catalogued for the sale and was predicted to attract one of the top bids, but he was withdrawn, reportedly due to a skin infection. There never had been any intention of selling Noor, which finished the year racing in the name of Howard's estate.

6

The Fastest Track in the Country

The Santa Anita and San Juan Capistrano Handicaps raised a number of questions about the relative merits of Noor and Citation in 1950, without providing satisfactory answers to any of them.

Was Noor as good as he seemed to be, or was he just a flash in the pan?

Could Noor beat Citation at level weights, or did he need help from a racing secretary?

Were Citation's best days really behind him, as some observers suggested?

Would the Calumet Farm star ever eclipse Stymie's earnings record or reach the million-dollar mark?

Some of the answers were waiting at Golden Gate Fields. The Northern California track would turn out to be a good place to settle the score, once and for all.

―――・◆・―――

Neither Noor nor Citation had raced since the March 4 San Juan Capistrano Handicap at Santa Anita, and the two horses arrived at Golden Gate Fields from nearby Tanforan fresh off two months' rest. Citation had come out of the San Juan Capistrano lame, and Noor had injured himself in a bizarre incident while prepping for the Tanforan

Handicap, but both horses were back in serious training for opening day at Golden Gate.

Citation returned to racing first, finishing second in a six-furlong allowance race on May 17. Citation was beaten by less than a length, and the winner, Roman In, had to equal the world record for the distance to do it. The clocking was a harbinger of record times to come. Cheap horses were turning in near-record times, and Jimmy Jones called Golden Gate's racing strip the fastest he'd ever seen. Just about everyone agreed with him.[100]

The next start for Citation, in two weeks, would be the Golden Gate Mile. Much better at longer distances than in sprints, Noor was sitting out the Mile.

"He needs more work before he's ready," Burley Parke explained, "and I'd hate to knock him out against those speed horses in the mile. He's responded very well since injuring himself prior to the Tanforan Handicap. We could have run him then, but perhaps he'd have been laid up for good."[101]

Noor was out of the Golden Gate Mile, but his absence didn't guarantee Citation an easy gallop in the race. His opponents included the crack sprinter Bolero, which a week earlier had set a new world record for six furlongs, $1:08^1/_5$.

"It seems the only way Cy can win again—and his next start's the Golden Gate Mile—is win and run in world record time himself," Jimmy Jones said.[102]

A tall order it was, and that's exactly what Citation did.

The horse dueled with Bolero from start to finish. Running head and head, they covered the first six furlongs of the mile in $1:07^3/_5$. That was three-fifths of a second *faster* than Bolero's week-old world record for the distance, but it wouldn't count as a new mark. Track records are based only on the final time for a race.

Carrying 128 pounds and conceding 5 pounds to Bolero, Citation won by three-quarters of a length and set a new world record for a mile, $1:33^3/_5$. The winner's share of the purse boosted Citation's career earnings to $924,630, past Stymie and into first place among the world's richest Thoroughbreds. Warren Wright's first objective for Citation was accomplished; only the elusive million-dollar mark remained.

Steve Brooks, who replaced veteran Eddie Arcaro after the Santa Anita Handicap, recalled some years later that he thought Citation came out of the Golden Gate Mile sore.

"I think his ankle was starting to hurt," Brooks said. "Jimmy said, 'He'll get over it in a day or two.' But Cy had come back, and he could now go out a winner without question, if he liked."[103]

A Miracle Year

Breeders of NOOR also Noor's sire
NASRULLAH
and dam
QUEEN of BAGHDAD

NOOR winning the Golden Gate Handicap

In four consecutive races, the Santa Anita Handicap, San Juan Capistrano Handicap, Forty Niner's Handicap and Golden Gate Handicap, Noor beat Citation and set up a new record time in each race.

After receiving weight from Citation in the first three races Noor conceded Citation 1 lb. in the Golden Gate Handicap and beat him in a new record time. In his fifth consecutive race Noor won the $50,000 American Handicap carrying top weight.

THE AGA KHAN'S STUDS

An advertisement for the Aga Khan's stud farms featured Noor's record-setting victory in the Golden Gate Handicap. *Courtesy of* Thoroughbred Times.

That wasn't going to happen.

The Golden Gate Handicap, the richest race of the meeting, was three weeks away, and Citation was coming off a world-record performance. Jimmy Jones began pointing Citation for the Golden Gate, with a stop on the way in the Forty Niners' Handicap. Citation would have to deal with Noor in both races.

Establishing Citation as racing's first millionaire had become a quest of sorts for Calumet owner Warren Wright, who was seventy-five years old and ailing. Charles Howard had been too ill to watch Noor beat Citation by the narrowest margin in the San Juan Capistrano Handicap, and he died before Noor raced again. Citation eventually would surpass the million-dollar mark, but Wright wouldn't be there to see it. Like Howard, Wright would succumb to illness and old age before the star of his stable reached a major milestone.

Brooks's concerns aside, there was little doubt about one thing: Citation might have lost a step or two since winning the Triple Crown two years earlier, but the horse still was good enough to race a mile faster than any other horse before him ever had. Jones had been correct when he speculated that Citation would have to run in world-record time to win the Golden Gate Mile. Now it looked as if it would take another world record to beat him.

Neither Burley Parke nor Jimmy Jones particularly wanted Noor and Citation to meet before the Golden Gate Handicap, but it was equally obvious to the two trainers that their horses needed a prep race. The Forty Niners' was it.[104]

Noor had trained brilliantly, coming within four-fifths of a second of the world record for one and one-eighth miles when he worked between races the week before the Forty Niners', but Parke said there was no excuse for a real race, and he dropped Noor's name into the entry box. Citation, Jones said, needed to race relatively often to stay fit.[105]

Noor again got weight from Citation for the one-and-one-eighth-mile Forty Niners', but the differential separating the two horses had narrowed again—128 pounds for Citation, 123 for Noor.

On Trust set the early pace in the Forty Niners', with Citation never far back in second. Noor broke slowly as usual and brought up the rear in the five-horse field. Jockey Steve Brooks moved Citation to the front after six furlongs, and the odds-on favorite still held a narrow lead at the top of the stretch. Noor was charging, though, and he caught Citation at the wire to win by a neck. The *Daily Racing Form* reported that "neither horse was unduly punished, but rather they were vigorously hand ridden" down the stretch.[106]

"I want to win with Noor and prove that his two previous wins over Citation were honestly earned," John Longden said before the Forty Niners'. "But this horse has not raced since the final day of the Santa Anita meeting and to abuse him would not be right."[107]

Noor beating Citation wasn't much of a surprise anymore; race-goers in California were becoming used to seeing the Howard stable's red and white silks in the winner's circle. What was truly amazing about the finish, especially considering that the horse wasn't under a hard drive from John Longden, was Noor's time—$1:46^{4}/_{5}$. Noor ran by Citation in the stretch without Longden ever using his whip, and the clocking still lowered the world record for one and one-eight miles by four-fifths of a second. Citation's official time for the race was the same as Noor's, an *unofficial* world record for the second-place finisher.

"Noor was, and is, too much horse," Jimmy Jones said after the race. "I don't think any other horse can beat Citation. Noor is just like a tornado."[108]

Walking back to the barn after the Forty Niners', Burley Parke looked ahead to Noor's next start.

"It was a tough spot," he said, "both for Jimmy and me. Neither of us wanted to run this race, especially. But the horses needed it, and the public expected it. What a race that'll be next Saturday."[109]

"Next Saturday" would be the Golden Gate Handicap, at a mile and a quarter. It wouldn't be the race everyone really wanted to see, because a match between Noor and Citation at level weights simply wasn't going to happen no matter how much the public demanded it. For the first time, though, Noor at 127 pounds would be conceding weight to Citation—1 pound.

Racing secretary Norris Royden justified his weights for the Golden Gate with high praise for both horses: "Noor is the only horse in the world that I know who could be asked to carry as much or more weight than Citation."[110]

The race marked Noor's first start of the season as the top weight and the first time since the 1948 Jockey Club Gold Cup, when three-year-old

Citation had carried 117 pounds to the older Phalanx's 124, that Citation had gotten weight from any horse.

The Golden Gate also marked the first time since Citation was a two-year-old in 1947 that he wasn't the betting favorite. The Golden Gate wasn't a match race because there were three other horses besides Noor and Citation among the starters, but the bettors treated it like one. A record crowd of 32,900 (the most people ever to attend a race in Northern California) made Noor the odds-on favorite to win the Golden Gate. Citation was the second choice at six to five.

For one minute and thirty-four seconds, the exact time it took for the pacesetter to run a mile, the Golden Gate Handicap looked less like the duel between Noor and Citation the crowd had come to see and more like a runaway for twenty-four-to-one long shot On Trust. Getting twenty-four pounds from Noor and twenty-three pounds from Citation, On Trust sprinted to the front at the start and built up a nine-length lead after a half mile. John Longden on Noor and Steve Brooks on Citation both were riding to instructions given them by their trainers and were content to let On Trust build an imposing lead unimpeded.[111]

On Trust still was in front at the top of the stretch, but he was tiring, his advantage had been cut to two lengths and he was no match for Noor. Slow away from the starting gate again and last during the early going, Noor charged by On Trust in the stretch and drew off to win by three lengths. Longden hit him just once, with a furlong to go.

"An insurance tap," Longden called it. Not that Noor needed one.

> *Noor's a champion. I never rode a horse who deserved that title any more, and I don't believe there's a living horse that can beat him. We had clear sailing all the way except that we were forced a bit wide into the stretch by Citation. Then he came on with power. I didn't touch him until we hit the eighth-pole, and that was just for insurance. It's a thrill to ride him.*[112]

Later, in the jockeys' room, Steve Brooks agreed.

"We just can't beat that horse, Johnny," Brooks told Longden. "He's just too good."[113]

Noor ran wide on the final turn and crossed the finish line well away from the rail. Losing that sort of ground in an important race often draws criticism for a jockey, but Burley Parke was happy with Longden's ride.

"All I told Johnny was for him to stay on the outside of Citation and to move when Citation moved," Parke said after the race. "I particularly cautioned him to not to get on the inside of Citation at any stage, and I had a strong reason for emphasizing this point." Just what that reason was, Parke never said.

Citation finished second, a length in front of On Trust, but he never challenged Noor.

Time for the one and one-quarter miles, 1:58^{1}/$_{5}$, was the fastest ever recorded for the distance. It was Noor's third world record in his last three starts, at distances ranging from one and one-eighth miles in the Forty Niners' Handicap to one and three-quarters miles in the San Juan Capistrano. Remarkably, two of Noor's world records came within a week of each other.

The Golden Gate Handicap marked a second defeat of sorts for Calumet Farm that day.

The previous world record for one and one-quarter miles (1:59^{4}/$_{5}$) had been shared by three horses, one of them Calumet's Coaltown. Both outstanding sons of leading sire Bull Lea, Citation and Coaltown had finished first and third in the 1948 Kentucky Derby. Coaltown then did much of the heavy lifting for Calumet when Citation was sidelined in 1949, winning twelve of fifteen races that year and sharing Horse of the Year honors with Capot.

Noor and Citation went their separate ways after the Golden Gate Handicap, Citation on a Southern Pacific train bound for Arlington Park in Chicago and Noor in a van headed south to Hollywood Park. Citation, as things turned out, would not run again in 1950. Rather than race the horse on an ankle that was becoming more problematic with every start, Jones sent Citation to Calumet Farm near Lexington, Kentucky. The ankle was fired, and Citation was put away for the rest of the year.[114]

Six months later, Citation was shipped back to Jimmy Jones in California for another try at becoming racing's first million-dollar earner. Citation won all three of his starts in 1951, taking the Century and American Handicaps before passing the million-dollar hurdle in the Hollywood Gold Cup on July 14. Another Calumet star, Bewitch, finished second in the Gold Cup, becoming racing's richest mare. Citation finally had done everything asked of him, and he was retired with a record of thirty-two victories from forty-five starts and career earnings of $1,085,760.

"As I look back," Jones recalled,

> *it probably would have been better had we not set a goal of being the first to win a million dollars. I feel I ran him* [Citation] *two or three times in quest of the million when possibly I shouldn't have. That's the way you win sometimes—chances have to be taken—but had Citation never run again after he received his injury in the Tanforan Handicap, his last start at three, his recognition of greatness would have been unlimited.*[115]

Like Charles Howard, who died before Noor fully established his reputation, Warren Wright did not live to see Citation's final races. The master of Calumet Farm died on December 31, 1950.

Years later, John Longden still bristled at the suggestion that beating Citation in 1950 didn't count for much.

After Longden hung up his tack and turned to training, he sometimes sent horses to Longacres outside Seattle, a track built and operated by a friend, Joe Gottstein. Turf writer Jon White worked at Longacres during the late 1970s, and one day he brought up the Noor/Citation rivalry.

"Each year from 1975 through 1980, Longacres was one of the tracks I worked at as a chart caller and columnist for the *Daily Racing Form*," White said.

> *One morning in the Longacres stable area, while gathering material for a column, I visited Longden's barn to chat with him about the horses he had stabled there. After he talked about those horses, I brought up the subject of Noor.*

A Miracle Year

> *"Noor was really a great horse," Longden said.*
>
> *With the knowledge that Citation's record in 1950 and 1951 paled in comparison to his record in 1947 and 1948, I then innocently said, "It's just too bad Citation was over the hill when he ran against Noor."*
>
> *"Over the hill?" Longden snapped. "Over the hill? That's bullshit. Noor had to break world or track records to beat Citation. If it took world or track records to beat Citation, how can you say Citation was over the hill?"*[116]

By the summer of 1950, Noor was the holder of world records for one and one-eighth miles (1:48$^{4}/_{5}$, in the Forty-Niners' Handicap), one and one-quarter miles (1:58$^{1}/_{5}$, in the Golden Gate Handicap) and one and three-quarters miles (2:52$^{4}/_{5}$, in the San Juan Capistrano Handicap), plus a Santa Anita track record for one and one-quarter miles (2:00, in the Santa Anita Handicap). Citation ran second in each of those races. The finish of the San Juan Capistrano was so close that Citation probably covered the one and three-quarters miles in world-record time as well.

Many easterners derided the records set over California's "pasteboard" tracks, and there were allegations that the Golden Gate racing strip had been specially prepared to generate world-record times. There was some circumstantial evidence in support of this—during forty-six days of racing at Golden Gate in 1950, races were run at eight different distances. Speed records were set at seven of them.[117]

Questions about the validity of the world records aside, the results speak for themselves. During a nineteen-week stretch, Noor faced Citation in five races and won four of them, even as the weights shifted in Citation's favor. Noor's domination over Citation was so unexpected that historians searched for an explanation that avoided an admission that during the spring of 1950 Noor was the better horse. William H.P. Robertson tried to sort things out this way:

> *The failure of these weight shifts to move up Citation, after the San Juan, has mystified turf followers ever since. One theory is that Noor for the first three races had been operating down below scale weight, where changes do not have much effect, while Citation was in the upper strata, where slight changes are magnified—a good horse scarcely notices the difference between, say, 115 and 122 pounds, but the difference between 129 and 131 can be telling. Another theory is that Noor was improving with each race while Citation was tailing off. Very likely, the explanation*

lies somewhere in between; Noor was unaffected by the first few weight changes, but by the time he moved up to scale weight, Citation could not take advantage of it.[118]

Jimmy Jones tended to eschew complicated theories about why Citation kept losing to Noor and instead found a simpler reason. "What a running, running son of a gun that Noor is," he said.[119]

No other explanation or excuse was needed.

7
Horse of the Year?

Burley Parke was a soft-spoken and unassuming man with a wonderful sense of humor, a well-respected trainer with a reputation for skill and patience in handling a difficult horse like Noor. From time to time, he would grouse about the weights racing secretaries put on his good horses, but questioning the competence and general intelligence of the track handicappers was a popular pastime on the backstretch then and now. Generally, though, Parke wasn't a man known to complain about things, at least not in public.

He watched Jimmy Jones spend the first half of 1950 between the proverbial rock and a hard place, facing pressure from his boss at Calumet Farm to keep chasing elusive money records with Citation when the trainer might have preferred a more conservative schedule for the horse. With the death of Charles Howard in June, Burley Parke found himself in a somewhat similar—and equally uncomfortable—position.

Over the years, Howard usually deferred to his trainers when it came to decisions about where and when to race the stable's horses. It was a measure of trust and respect on Howard's part, and it was an essential element of the way he ran all of his businesses. Parke still was in charge of the stable after Howard's death, but now he was training for a committee that included Marcella Howard and sons Lindsey, Robert and Charles Jr. In the weeks following Howard's death, it wasn't exactly clear what plans were in place for Noor.

The horse was nominated for a trio of stakes races at Hollywood Park, but the van ride downstate from Golden Gate Fields apparently didn't sit

Trainers H.A. (Jimmy) Jones, Judge Cassidy, Bill Winfrey and Burley Parke. *Courtesy of the Parke family.*

well with Noor's finicky constitution. A notoriously poor shipper, he missed the first two engagements and wound up not racing for a month after his record-setting performance in the Golden Gate Handicap. For an otherwise healthy horse that had set two world records seven days apart, a month was a significant amount of down time.

"I thought we should wait a little longer before he starts at Hollywood Park," the trainer explained at the time.

> *After he shipped down from the north, he went slightly off his feed for about three days. It wasn't anything serious and I think it might have been some new hay we had here for him, or the change of water.*
>
> *We got his old hay back and started to give him distilled water and now Noor is back in fine shape and doing well. However, I don't want to rush him until I'm sure he's good and strong again.*[120]

Carrying 132 pounds, Noor defeats Dharan in the American Handicap. *Courtesy of Thoroughbred Times.*

When Noor did get back to the races, for the one-and-one-quarter-mile American Handicap in late July, he produced another spectacular performance. Assigned top weight of 132 pounds, the most he ever would carry in his four years of racing, Noor wore down Dharan in the last furlong to win by a half length. Conceding a whopping 32 pounds to Dharan, Noor won in 2:00^1/5, one-fifth of a second off the track record.

Noor was under a hard drive through the stretch, a classic riding effort by the Pumper. After the race, jockey John Longden said that it was the first time he'd found it necessary to use his whip repeatedly.

"He didn't want to pass Dharan," said Longden, who was critical of Noor's 132-pound impost. "I guess he was getting a little tired under that weight."[121]

There was little chance that second-place finisher Dharan tired under his weight, a feather-light one hundred pounds. Jockey Nick Wall, who came to California from New York specifically for the mount on Dharan, was one of a handful of riders who actually could make weight at one hundred pounds. Champion rider in 1938, when his mounts won ninety-seven races

Burley Parke and Noor, with jockey John Longden, in the winner's circle after the American Handicap. *Courtesy of the Parke family.*

and earned $385,161, Wall had been Seabiscuit's nemesis in the late 1930s. He won the 1937 Bowie Handicap with Esposa, the 1938 Santa Anita Handicap with Stagehand and the 1938 Laurel Stakes with Jacola, all the wins coming as upsets at the expense of Seabiscuit.

Word went out from the Howard camp *before* the American Handicap that it would be Noor's last race in California.[122] Those plans were tempered *after* the American, when Marcella Howard said that Noor might run again in California after all.

"It all depends on what goes on in the east and how much weight they keep piling on Noor," she said. "After all, there must be a limit. If this goes on, Noor probably will be retired."[123]

"The east" Marcella was talking about involved a brief campaign planned for Noor in New York. Longden thought the weight-for-age races on the East Coast "would just be made to order" for Noor,[124] but Burley Parke wasn't so sure. It wasn't the competition awaiting Noor in New York that gave Parke pause. Instead, it was the prospect of journeying across the country with a horse that didn't care much for travel.

Burley Parke and Noor with a blanket commemorating the American Handicap. *Courtesy of Betfair Hollywood Park.*

"It has taken me long months to get to understand this horse," Parke said. "He will not stand constant honing. Once you get him to a perfect edge—and I think he has that edge now—you have to be careful with him. He is the kind of horse that will lose his edge through long travel. But if Mrs. Howard wants to ship him to New York, I'll go along with the plans."[125]

Seabiscuit had shipped all over the country a few years earlier, and it is not known whether the success of those excursions prompted the decision to send Noor east. If so, some fundamental differences in temperament between the two horses weren't taken into account. Seabiscuit proved to be a good traveler, often riding in a roomy Pullman car outfitted specially for him, and he generally spent his time eating and sleeping.[126] Noor, on the other hand, was a terrible traveler, and sending him on a cross-country trip was very problematic.

Parke recognized that. He didn't like the idea of dispatching Noor on an East Coast invasion, not with numerous attractive opportunities for the horse in California, but in the end he acquiesced. He gave Noor a few days' rest at Hollywood Park and then loaded the horse on a train bound for Saratoga in upstate New York.

Noor's East Coast campaign started badly, and then things got worse.

He developed a cough after the American Handicap that delayed his shipping across country until early in August. Noor finally arrived in Saratoga several days later, on August 11, in time for some of the weight-for-age races that Longden was excited about. The cough persisted, however, and Noor's training was interrupted to such an extent that he missed the entire Saratoga meeting. The horse eventually made his New York debut in a mid-September overnight handicap at Belmont Park.

Noor carried 128 pounds in that race and lost to Greentree Stable's One Hitter. Described by one writer as a "tough little son of Shut Out, who was a menace to any horse when the weight was right,"[127] One Hitter got 21 pounds from Noor and won by one and a quarter lengths. The winning time was three-fifths of a second off the Belmont Park track record for one and one-sixteenth miles.

The weight apparently was right again five days later. Getting eighteen pounds from Noor at one and a half miles, One Hitter won the Manhattan Handicap by a neck. Calumet's Ponder finished third. Losing to a longshot twice in succession was bad enough; worse was that Noor had raced on even terms with One Hitter through part of the stretch in the Manhattan but couldn't close the deal when it counted.

Noor wrapped up his East Coast adventure with a third loss, this time to Kentucky Derby winner Hill Prince in the weight-for-age Jockey Club Gold Cup. Carrying scale weight of 117 pounds to Noor's 124, Hill Prince was in front by eight lengths during the early going and never was challenged. Eased at the finish, he won by four lengths over favored Noor, covering the two miles in $3:23^2/5$.

Noor's supporters, like Citation's earlier in the year, now found themselves in the unusual position of having to explain, and maybe excuse, Noor's defeats. The racing strip at Belmont Park was a common culprit. Tracks in California tended to be hard and fast, while horses at Belmont Park were running over a sandy, deeper surface. Noor might have had problems adapting to the new footing, plus he had a tendency to "run down" behind

A Miracle Year

Noor at Belmont Park in the fall of 1950. *Courtesy of* Thoroughbred Times.

at Belmont. The horse came out of the Jockey Club Gold Cup with both hind heels abraded by the sand and bleeding, despite Parke's best efforts at protecting those areas with layers of bandages.[128]

One writer even went so far as to suggest that Noor fared poorly in New York because the "humid heat depressed him." Noor was raised in a cooler climate, the writer added, and the "fog and rain of the San Francisco region was right down his alley. It rains quite a bit in Eire."[129]

Weather-challenged or not, Noor returned to California after the Jockey Club Gold Cup, arriving at Hollywood Park in late October.

Writer Joe H. Palmer summed up the ill-fated East Coast excursion this way: "He added nothing to his reputation, little to his earnings, though he got some compliments on his appearance."[130]

To his credit, and as expected, Burley Parke made no excuses for Noor. Parke didn't need any, according to Palmer, who said "his horse was beaten twice by weight and once by the best horse of the year."[131]

Palmer was referring to Hill Prince as the season's best horse, and according to a couple of separate year-end polls, he was right. Hill Prince was selected as Horse of the Year in voting conducted by the *Daily Racing Form* and by the Thoroughbred Racing Associations.

Noor was passed over for Horse of the Year honors, but he wasn't ignored entirely by the voters, who named him Champion Handicap Horse in both polls. The problem was, voting for both of the so-called year-end polls actually took place in November, well *before* the end of the year. Both Noor and Hill Prince had more racing ahead of them before the 1950 season really wound down. Naming Hill Prince as Horse of the Year prematurely was like announcing the winner of the World Series in the eighth inning of the deciding game.

Back on familiar ground in California, Noor was unbeatable.

He made his first post-Belmont start in the Westwood Purse, an overnight allowance race on December 1. The five-horse field for the Westwood was short on numbers but long on class. In addition to Noor, the top weight under 124 pounds, the race attracted Palestinian (third in Ponder's 1949 Kentucky Derby and a multiple stakes winner on the East Coast) and Assault (like Citation a winner of the Triple Crown, Assault's sweep coming in 1946). Noor was conceding 4 pounds to Palestinian and a dozen to Assault, a seven-year-old that was attempting a comeback after being away from the races for thirteen months.

Assault was the enigma in the Westwood field. The horse was dominant at three in 1946, when he won the Triple Crown and was Horse of the Year for his breeder Robert J. Kleberg Jr.'s King Ranch. He won five straight races the next year as a four-year-old, successfully carrying 130 pounds or more in the Brooklyn, Suburban and Butler Handicaps, before losing a much-publicized match race with Armed. Bothered by a laundry list of injuries that finally took their toll, Assault was retired to stud at King Ranch in Texas. He was an abject failure as a breeding stallion, however, and he was put back in training.[132]

Assault won impressively in his first start after he returned to the races, but questions remained about how good he really was, at his age, after a

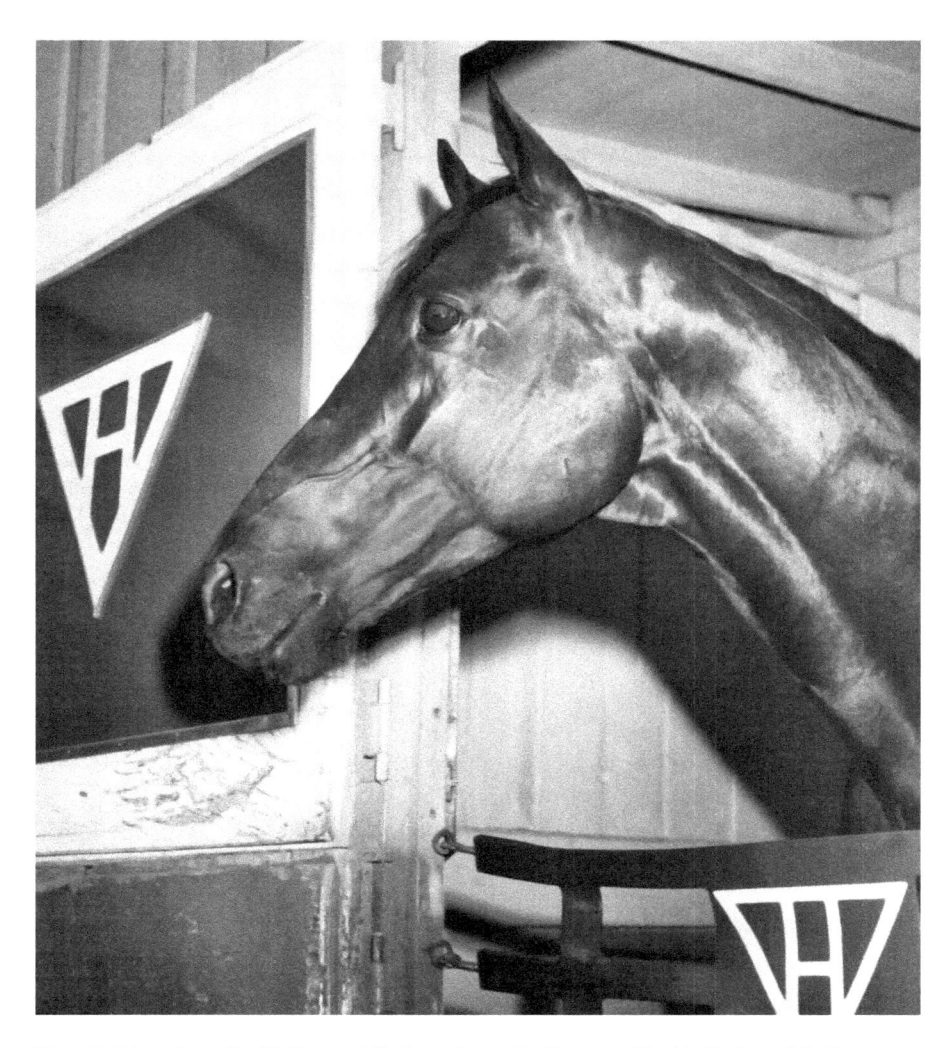

Noor in his stall on the Hollywood Park backstretch. *Courtesy of Betfair Hollywood Park.*

Finish and winner's circle photographs from the Westwood Purse. *Courtesy of the Parke family.*

long layoff. It must have seemed like "déjà vu all over again"[133] for Noor's supporters, who had fielded similar questions about the longevity of Citation's ability earlier in the year.

Noor dawdled through the first half mile of the Westwood while Palestinian and Assault vied for the early lead; then, on the final turn, John Longden moved the favorite up and out to the middle of the track. Despite racing very wide and losing substantial ground in the process, Noor was three lengths in front at the top of the stretch. He drew off with very little urging from Longden to win by seven lengths. Palestinian was second, and Assault was third. Noor set a track record for one and one-eighths miles, winning in 1:48.

With his victory in the Westwood, Noor became the first horse in history to defeat two Triple Crown winners—Citation in the spring and Assault in the fall. It was a feat that would not be duplicated for twenty-eight years, not until Exceller won the Marlboro Cup at the expense of back-to-back Triple Crown winners Seattle Slew (1977) and Affirmed (1978). Taking into account the dearth of Triple Crown winners since the 1970s, the odds of another horse even meeting—let alone defeating—two Triple Crown winners are almost nonexistent.

"He's a different horse than he ever showed back East," Burley Parke said of Noor after the Westwood, "and perhaps he is better than at any time in

A Miracle Year

his career."[134] Noor would need to be; he'd face the best field of the year in his next start.

———•◆•———

Whether the 1950 Hollywood Gold Cup actually was the best race of the year remains a matter of opinion, with Noor's San Juan Capistrano Handicap and maybe a few others also legitimate contenders for that distinction. Undeniable, however, was the Gold Cup's status as the richest race run anywhere in the world in 1950, with $100,000 guaranteed to the winner.

A few other races that year offered six-figure purses—Noor's Santa Anita Handicap, the Santa Anita Derby, the Santa Anita Maturity and the Kentucky Derby among them—but none of those races had a winner's share of the total purse that exceeded the Gold Cup's guaranteed return of $100,000. Not surprisingly, the Gold Cup drew a field commensurate with its generous purse:

- Noor—multiple stakes winner, victor over Citation and Assault, handicap champion (odds-on favorite)
- Hill Prince—Kentucky Derby winner, Horse of the Year, conqueror of Noor (four-to-one second choice)
- Ponder—Kentucky Derby winner, leading money winner in 1949 (five-to-one third choice)
- Next Move—champion three-year-old filly (odds of ten to one)
- Great Circle—generally regarded as the best three-year-old in California in 1950 (odds of twenty-four to one)
- Palestinian—East Coast stakes winner (odds of thirty-seven to one)
- Assault—Triple Crown winner and Horse of the Year (odds of thirty-eight to one)
- On Trust—One of the best California-breds of his time (odds of forty-six to one)

The race attracted a top-notch field for two vastly different reasons: the unmatched purse and, ironically, a disaster that occurred at the track some eighteen months earlier.

Late in the night on May 5, 1949, a fire of undetermined origin tore through the Hollywood Park grandstand and clubhouse, reducing the entire structure to smoldering rubble. At the time, the conflagration was thought to be the largest fire in Southern California and possibly the largest grandstand fire ever in this country.

The fire came only two weeks before the Hollywood Park meeting was supposed to begin, but racing started on schedule anyway, with Santa Anita acting as a stand-in. Delays in rebuilding the facility resulted in a split meeting at Hollywood Park the next year, 1950, with twenty days run during the summer and an additional thirty days scheduled for the winter. Noor won the American Handicap during the summer session; the winter portion of the card, which included the rich Hollywood Gold Cup, attracted a number of prominent stables that shipped to California rather than to Florida, where the purses were much smaller.

Attendance and betting were down during the winter days, but the quality of racing was stellar.[135]

Some horses prefer their races close together, while others thrive when their starts are spaced out. Noor was one of those rare Thoroughbreds that could turn in world-record performances with little rest between his races or win just as convincingly when he raced only every month or so. In that regard, the horse was a perfect match for Burley Parke, who had a knack for bringing Noor up to peak condition either on races run in succession or with a series of carefully planned workouts. Taking into account all the factors—the two-month hiatus since the Jockey Club Gold Cup in New York, a series of quick works and a win that came within one-fifth of a second of the track record a week before the Hollywood Gold Cup—and Noor figured to be at the top of his game.

John Longden had been one of Noor's staunchest supporters ever since he picked up the mount on the horse nearly a year earlier at Tanforan, and he was supremely confident prior to the Gold Cup.

"Noor is at his peak now and he will win for sure," the diminutive rider predicted in the paddock before the race.[136]

For the first three-quarters of a mile, though, Longden's confidence—and that of the bettors who made his mount the odds-on favorite—looked grossly misplaced.

Noor (#8, left) breaks from the outside at the start of the Hollywood Gold Cup. *Courtesy of Betfair Hollywood Park.*

The starter sent the field away quickly, a scant thirty seconds or so after the last horse had stepped into the starting gate. That last horse in the gate happened to be Noor, and the start seemed to catch the horse by surprise. He broke awkwardly from the outside post position and was crowded by Hill Prince to his left, and for a stride or two Longden looked off balance, struggling to get into a comfortable position low over Noor's withers. The filly Next Move sprinted to the front as everyone expected, and she set a fast pace for six furlongs. Noor and Hill Prince were out of touch and trailed the leaders by such a great margin that they sometimes dropped out of the frame in the grainy Universal Newsreel films of the race.

With a half mile to go, Next Move still was in front, but Palestinian was gaining ground. John Longden on Noor and Eddie Arcaro on Hill Prince were moving on the leaders and were about to make decisions that would shape the outcome of the Gold Cup.

Midway through the final turn, Longden pulled Noor to the outside to avoid the traffic jam that was developing in front of him. At the same time, Arcaro cut to the inside to save ground with Hill Prince. Noor wound up in the clear; Hill Prince didn't. The opening Arcaro thought he saw on the rail

Next Move leads going into the first turn in the Hollywood Gold Cup. Noor (far left) is next-to-last. *Courtesy of Betfair Hollywood Park.*

vanished in an instant, and he was forced to check Hill Prince and go around the slower horses.

By the time Arcaro got Hill Prince in the clear and running again, Noor had passed him and was taking aim on Palestinian. With Longden whipping for all he was worth through the stretch, Noor outran Palestinian and won by a length. Hill Prince passed a tiring Next Move to finish third. Time for the one and one-quarter miles, 1:59^4/$_5$, was another track record for Noor.

Burley Parke had confidence in John Longden's judgment, and he often gave the rider few, if any, instructions before a race. The Hollywood Gold Cup was an exception.

"That was one race that was run exactly as we had planned," Parke said the day after the Gold Cup.

> *Johnny Longden and I had gone over every inch of it beforehand. The horses I was most concerned about were Hill Prince and Ponder. I told Johnny never to let Hill Prince get too much of a lead on him in the early part of the race. We wanted to be not more than three—or four,*

A Miracle Year

On the backstretch of the Gold Cup, Next Move still is in front. Racing in the middle of the track, Noor has moved up to fifth. *Courtesy of Betfair Hollywood Park.*

It's Next Move, Palestinian and Noor coming into the stretch. *Courtesy of Betfair Hollywood Park.*

> at the most—lengths off Hill Prince down the backstretch. He is a great colt, and you can't give him any more than that, or you'll never catch him.
>
> As for Ponder [fifth in the Gold Cup], he is a real bulldog. When Ponder catches a horse by the head, he never gives up. He just wears you into the ground. If Ponder came up to him, Johnny had instructions to use *Noor as much as necessary to get in the clear again. As it turned out, Ponder did not run his race, and I knew *Noor wasn't going to lose when he caught and passed Hill Prince on the turn.[137]

After the race, Arcaro suggested that he might have ridden the race differently if he had been aware that Noor was going to be retired afterward:

A Miracle Year

Finish of the Hollywood Gold. *Courtesy of Betfair Hollywood Park.*

> *If I had known that Hill Prince would never again have a chance to meet *Noor, I believe I would have ridden the race differently. Coming into the last quarter, I would have gone to the outside with Hill Prince, instead of trying to get through that hole that closed up, and the result would have been a photo-finish.*
>
> *But I have never ridden the safe way. I've always taken chances if I thought I could save some ground, and I've been lucky. This time I wasn't. I felt I had to save some ground in the Gold Cup with Hill Prince because at the weights—giving *Noor six pounds on the scale—I wasn't at all sure I had the better horse.*[138]

Noor was a convincing winner, and a strong argument can be made that he would have been the logical choice for Horse of the Year honors if voting had been held after the Gold Cup rather than before. Fans of Hill Prince, on the other hand, could hang their hypothetical hats on the weights the two horses carried. This might sound odd because both horses shared top weight of 130 pounds, but based on the theoretical weight-for-age scale, Hill Prince really was conceding 6 pounds to his older rival. That was the weight disadvantage Eddie Arcaro was talking about.

A plaque commemorating Noor's 1950 Hollywood Gold Cup. *Courtesy of Betfair Hollywood Park.*

Scale weight for five-year-old Noor in December was 126 pounds; scale for three-year-old Hill Prince was 120. Factoring in the weights the two horses actually carried, 130 pounds, Noor was only 4 pounds above scale, while Hill Prince was 10 pounds over. Subtract Noor's 4 pounds from Hill Prince's 10, and by scale, the Horse of the Year was conceding 6 pounds to his older rival.

Some writers felt that the theoretical scale-weight differential, rather than the fact that Noor and Hill Prince actually carried equal weight in the Hollywood Gold Cup, was the deciding factor in determining which of the two should be Horse of the Year. By this somewhat convoluted logic, Hill Prince's win in the Jockey Club Gold Cup (with Noor second) trumped Noor's convincing win over Hill Prince in California, and the latter result wouldn't have affected the voting.[139] Further support for Hill Prince as Horse of the Year was his season-ending victory under 128 pounds in the Sunset Handicap.

For racing fans not inclined toward higher math, or those lacking a slide rule to figure all this out, the Horse of the Year dilemma was a much simpler proposition: Noor beat Hill Prince fair and square in the richest race of the year, carrying the same weight and racing over the same track.

A Miracle Year

Joe H. Palmer, a vocal and humorous critic of what he considered the artificially fast tracks in California and a strong supporter of Hill Prince as Horse of the Year, made a similar point about Noor's Hollywood Gold Cup in the *Blood-Horse*:

> *I am not at all impressed by the fact that he ran the distance in 1:59⁴/₅, because California tracks are downhill all the way, as I've said before. But I am impressed by the fact that he beat an extremely good field, giving weight to all except Hill Prince, and that, whatever the speed of the tracks, he gets over them faster than anything else.*

Burley Parke met Noor and John Longden on the track in front of the new grandstand. The trainer laid a hand on the reins and led the horse into the winner's circle as more than fifty thousand fans roared their approval. Longden doffed his riding helmet to the crowd, and a heavy blanket of yellow flowers was draped across Noor's withers.

The scene in the winner's circle was charged with emotion.

Charles Howard was dead, gone before he had an opportunity to see Noor develop into the successor to Seabiscuit he so desperately wanted. Most of Howard's horses had been auctioned, and Noor was being retired at the top of his form, a rarity in any sport. Marcella Howard was almost speechless. And Burley Parke, who had previously announced that he was taking a break from training, was following Noor into retirement.

"I've been doing a lot of thinking about that," Parke told Robert Hebert of the *Blood-Horse* the day before the race,

> *and I guess it might be a good idea if *Noor and I left the races together. I haven't had a real vacation for about 30 years. It was a real pleasure working for Mr. Howard, and later for Mrs. Marcella Howard, but I don't think she would mind if I asked to leave now. After this race, I would like to take a vacation—for about a year.*[140]

Of all the people in the winner's circle, though, John Longden may have been the most affected. When the photographers were finished with their work, an attendant pulled the flowers off. Longden leaned forward out of the saddle, buried his face in Noor's mane and wrapped his arms around the horse's neck.

"*Noor is a very affectionate horse," Burley Parke said later,

> *and we have always made it a habit to speak kindly to him. In the winner's circle, when Johnny leaned over and kissed *Noor on the neck, and we all patted him and rubbed his head, and folks were talking kindly to him and saying, "Fine going, old boy!"—well, I could not help but feel that *Noor understood it all, and that he knew he had done something that was very nice. I had a feeling, too, that *Noor sensed that this was the end.*[141]

8
Retirement

Noor won the Hollywood Gold Cup in spectacular fashion, and when he came out of the race sound and apparently ready to run again, there was some pressure to keep the horse in training. Another rich race, the Santa Anita Handicap, was coming up in a few weeks, and a return engagement for Noor would have been a coup for track management. Even the possibility of a match race with Hill Prince, which was very unlikely to happen under any circumstances, was bandied about in the local newspapers.

Marcella Howard put to rest any doubts that might have lingered about plans for Noor. She telephoned J.F. MacKenzie, general manager of Hollywood Park, on Thursday after the Gold Cup and asked him to forward a message to the press:

> *For some time we had planned the definite retirement of Noor after the Hollywood Gold Cup. After the race last Saturday, we reiterated that this would be his last competition on the track.*
>
> *Since last summer the horse has been required to carry very high weight, and, as we have said before, we believe the proper time to retire him is when he is at his peak and before there is a chance of his being over-raced at high weight and caused to lose his best form or break down.*
>
> *Noor has already been taken out of training. His racing plates have been removed and he will be vanned to the ranch at San Ysidro tomorrow, Friday. We do not believe it would serve any good purpose for him to be put back in training now for any kind of a race.*[142]

And that was that.

Noor was retired as planned. His combined career record, from two years racing in England and another two years in the United States, was twelve wins from thirty-one starts, six second-place finishes and six third-place finishes. His earnings in this country totaled $356,940, all but $10,000 of that total accumulated during his 1950 campaign, and he was the leading money winner of the year. Noor picked up an additional £6,699 racing in England. Taking into account potential problems with converting foreign currency, the *Daily Racing Form* calculated his career earnings at $394,863.

Noor entered stud in 1951 in California. He was moved to Kentucky for the 1952–54 breeding seasons, standing at Charles A. Kenney's Springside Farm. The horse then was returned to California, to Lindsay Howard's Binglin Stable near Moorpark.

On his breeding, race record and conformation, Noor should have attracted the attention of some of the country's leading breeders. Why he did not is a mystery.

Noor's sire, Nasrullah, would turn out to be one of the most influential stallions of the twentieth century, and Noor was one of the first of Nasrullah's sons to enter stud in this country. A leading sire in England and Ireland, Nasrullah was the leading sire of two-year-olds when his first North American crop reached the races in 1954, and he would top the general sire list five times, in 1955, 1956, 1959, 1960 and 1962.[143] For a breeder with a nice mare who couldn't get to Nasrullah, a champion son of the stallion should have been a strong second choice.

Strangely, however, Noor's books were relatively small, and the mares sent to him over the years often were not the best. His crops exceeded twenty foals only five times, and only once did he have as many as twenty-four registered foals in a single year. By the early 1960s, Noor was being bred to only a handful of mares each year.

Noor proved to be a good sire, but not a great one. From nineteen crops, he sired a total of 254 registered foals. Of those, 208 made it to the races, and 139, a little more than half, were winners. Noor's offspring earned $3,073,732, an average of $14,778 for each starter. That translates into an Average-Earnings Index of 1.39, which is better than the average earnings of all stallions with progeny racing during the same time period as runners sired by Noor.[144]

He sired thirteen stakes winners, probably the best of which was Noble Noor, winner of the $100,000 Hollywood Juvenile Championship in 1959 and the California Derby in 1960. Noble Noor was touted for a time as the

West Coast's best hope for the 1960 Kentucky Derby, but he was injured while defeating T.V. Lark in the California Derby, and he didn't make the trip to Churchill Downs. Noble Noor was Noor's leading money winner, with a career total of $169,850.

Noor's other stakes winners were: In Reserve (foaled in 1952, a multiple stakes winner in California and Noor's leading winning filly); Nooran (1952); Prince Noor (1952); Noorsage (1953); Joe Price (1954); Noureddin (1955, winner of the Olympic Handicap and second or third in ten other stakes, including the 1958 Kentucky Derby and Wood Memorial); Ten Five (1956); Noble Noor (1957); Flutterby (1958); Bounding Main (1959); Yours (1961, a multiple stakes winner in France); Zulu Lad (1962); and Lar's Theme (1966).

Noor also developed something of a reputation for siring durable horses that seemingly could run forever.

Diamond Jubilee raced for nine years during the late 1950s and early 1960s, winning eighteen times from an astonishing 191 starts and setting a track record at Detroit Race Course. Three other horses sired by Noor chalked up more than 150 starts, and four others raced more than one hundred times each during lengthy careers.

Noor's Image, from the horse's second crop of foals, wasn't the best of Noor's progeny, but she certainly proved to be the most interesting. She won twice and ran second in a pair of important stakes races for juvenile fillies in 1955, and at the end of the season she was ranked in the top tier of the year's best two-year-olds. Noor's Image never won again, and she finished her career in cheap company, running against $5,000 claimers.

The late Peter Fuller picked her up for that price in 1958 and a few years later bred the mare to Horse of the Year Native Dancer. It was an odd choice of stallions for an inexpensive broodmare with little in the way of a produce record. Native Dancer's stud fee was $20,000, the highest in the world, and Noor's Image had produced only one modest stakes winner. The foal produced from that mating was Dancer's Image, a gray colt with questionable ankles that made racing history—and not in a good way.

Dancer's Image finished first in the 1968 Kentucky Derby, a clear winner over the favorite, Calumet Farm's Forward Pass. The victory was short-lived, however, when post-race urine tests apparently were positive for phenylbutazone, a pain killer that was prohibited under the Rules of Racing in Kentucky. Fuller challenged the efficacy of the tests and the competence of the state chemist who evaluated the results, losing before the Churchill Downs stewards and the state racing commission, winning in Franklin Circuit Court and then losing again in the Kentucky Court of Appeals.

Five years and a quarter-million dollars in legal fees later, Dancer's Image was disqualified, and the winner's share of the purse and the $5,000 gold trophy were awarded to Calumet Farm. Dancer's Image was the first, and remains the only, Kentucky Derby winner to be disqualified.[145]

Noor's popularity declined rapidly during the late 1960s. After he was retired from stud duty, he was pensioned at Loma Rica Ranch on the outskirts of Grass Valley in Northern California, where he spent his last years. Noor was euthanized on November 16, 1974, at the age of twenty-nine. He was buried in an unmarked grave in the infield of the training track at Loma Rica. Conqueror of Triple Crown winners Citation and Assault, holder of several world records, and a champion handicap horse himself, Noor had slipped out of racing's collective consciousness by the mid-1970s. His death merited only three lines in the "Late Items" section of the *Blood-Horse* magazine.[146]

Largely forgotten for forty years, Noor would return to prominence only through an unlikely confluence of people and events.

PART II
OLD FRIENDS

9
Loma Rica

It was about 2:30 in the afternoon on a hot day in August when the backhoe turned up the first piece of bone. At least it looked like bone, smooth with a grayish-white color when all the dirt was cleaned off, and a piece of bone is what everyone desperately wanted it to be. But the day already had been marred by false starts and dashed hopes. A miasma of resignation was setting in, and the small group of people at the excavation site was understandably wary of another disappointment.[147]

It's easy to mistake slivers of rock or petrified wood for pieces of bone. They all look more or less alike to the untrained eye, and there were a lot of untrained eyes at Loma Rica Ranch that day. There are sophisticated laboratory tests to distinguish bone from most other materials that might show up in a burial site, but there's an easier way. It's an old trick well known to field archaeologists everywhere.

Touch the unknown sample to the tip of your tongue—if it sticks, it's bone.[148]

Gary Parke, one of Burley Parke's sons, was the first person to spot what appeared to be a bone lying in a bucketful of dirt pulled up by the backhoe. He handed it on to Erin Dwyer, one of two archaeologists providing professional advice and assistance.

Dwyer examined the relic Parke had found and was confident she was holding a piece of bone in her hand. Then she touched it to the tip of her tongue.

It stuck to her tongue, confirming that it was, in fact, a piece of bone.

Charlotte Farmer recalled the events of that day:

Above: The exhumation of Noor's remains at Loma Rica Ranch.
Courtesy of Denise Jaffke.

Left: Noor and Burley Park.
Courtesy of the Parke family.

It is now sometime around 2:30 p.m. I try to sit, can't. Walk back out... The air is grim. Rocky walks over to me and tells me her father's spirit will help us find ✲Noor and to, once again, have faith.

Then I hear, "We have a bone."

I yell out in the direction of those standing in the shade, "We have him, we have him!" and begin to sob uncontrollably. Burley's granddaughter grabs me, and I cannot stop crying. They don't understand the crying; it is not sadness but relief.

We found him.

My mind is awash with what if we hadn't found him this day—the donations, the timeline, the news media. A one-day delay would have been disastrous on so many levels, but I would have dug up the entire upper quadrant of the track to find him, and I know Erin would have been right there with me. Throughout this day, Erin keeps reassuring me that she wouldn't give up until he is found.

Everyone rushes out from the shade over to the hole. They have brought shovels and trowels and begin going through the dirt.

I stay away from the site.

I hear we have a horseshoe; we have another bone.

It keeps going on.

Everyone is ecstatic, smiling and chattering... For me it is a blur filled with sounds. At this point the sun has done its damage. I am beginning to get heat exhaustion as I had years earlier in Palm Springs. Don't care; I'm not getting in the shade.

I just stand there and stare.[149]

All this happened on Friday, August 26, 2011.

The work took place at Loma Rica Ranch, a Northern California farm about a mile east of Grass Valley. Loma Rica is where Noor spent his last years as a pensioner, until his death in 1974.

Against all odds, they found him.

It was the end of one journey for Noor and the start of another.

Charlotte Farmer is a "Kelso girl" through and through, and who can blame her? It's difficult not to be a fan of the gallant gelding. He raced eight seasons, won thirty-nine races competing against several generations of top runners and established a record for career earnings of $1,977,896. Scores of horses have won more money than Kelso since he set the mark—he doesn't even rank among the top fifty richest Thoroughbreds now—but nearly $2 million was serious money in the 1960s.

Kelso was named Horse of the Year five consecutive times, a feat no other horse has come close to matching. Upon his retirement in 1966, the *Blood-Horse* had this to say: "Kelso demonstrated the durability of class. No horse in our time was so good, for so long. His was mature greatness."[150]

Charlotte is an equal-opportunity racing enthusiast, though, and when a horse, or a trainer, or an owner or a jockey snags her attention, it triggers a frenzy of research. Knowing a little is never good enough.

A longtime fan of Charles Howard and Seabiscuit, Farmer started visiting author Laura Hillenbrand's website in 2003.[151] She printed anything of interest she came across and spent some time swapping her Kelso stories for other people's reminiscences of Howard and Seabiscuit.

Four years later, while clearing a stack of papers off her desk, Farmer came across an e-mail she had printed from Gae Seal, a reader who was asking Hillenbrand questions about Noor and wondering how to research the "post-Seabiscuit days."[152] Seal lived near Loma Rica, and she was interested because of a proposed development project that looked as if it might threaten the property and Noor's grave.

Charlotte lives north of Grass Valley in Redding, a drive of about two hours. She didn't know anything about Noor at the time, and she didn't have much interest in the horse. For a woman who believes that no good question goes unanswered, though, a closer look came without much prodding:

> *That fateful day as I looked at Gae's inquiry, I thought, "How hard can this be to answer this lady's question?"*
>
> *I had done quite a bit of research into C.S. Howard and his world, so I tracked down Gae's phone number, and we*

spoke. She gave me what information she had, and from there I proceeded to see what I could come up with by way of answers.

What was Loma Rica, and who was *Noor?

I had heard the name along with Midland and the obvious Seabiscuit and Kayak II, but how would anything owned by C.S. Howard make it that far north? I decided I needed to find out if anyone was still alive from that period with regard to the ranch. The first thing that came to mind was that a horse ranch would need a veterinarian. That would be a good starting place, so I got ahold of the Grass Valley Chamber of Commerce and spoke with Judy Foy. I told her my story and asked if there were any veterinarians in the area who might still be around from the 1960s and who would know something about Loma Rica.

She suggested I call Dr. Jon Peek, a local veterinarian, who is now retired. She knew he had been in the area for many years, and he might be able to steer me in the right direction as to who to talk with. She gave me the number to his veterinary practice, and I thanked her.

I called the number given, and when the receptionist answered, I asked if I could speak with Dr. Peek. I told her this was not business but that I had some questions and was told by the chamber of commerce he might be able to answer them. She said she would check with the doctor to see if he had time to talk with me and put me on hold.

You gotta love this next part. It was as if fate had stepped in. While I was on hold, they had music playing. It was from the 1930s, and the singer was Bing Crosby. Bing Crosby, C.S. Howard's good friend. I thought, this is fate; I am going to find out something.

Dr. Peek, it turned out, was about as good a first contact as Farmer could have found to begin her search for information about Noor. He had been one of the local veterinarians who cared for the horses at Loma Rica. He also was the vet who euthanized Noor and had some knowledge about where the horse was buried in the infield of the training track. He suggested that Farmer contact Roxann Freitas, "Rocky" to her friends, the daughter of the late Henry Freitas. Manager of Loma Rica for thirty-seven years, Henry Freitas had selected the burial site for Noor.

Rocky proved to be a "delight," according to Farmer. While she had not been at the farm the day Noor was buried, she was a wealth of information about Loma Rica.

Farmer made the first of her many trips to the farm in late October 2007, in the company of Dr. Peek and Rocky Freitas. Meeting them at Loma Rica was Nell Scannon, vice-president of communication outreach for Carville Sierra, Inc. Scannon's stepfather, Phil Carville, was the principal developer of the Loma Rica property and an important cog in Farmer's plan. All she had in mind at the time was locating Noor's grave so that the horse and his final resting place could be recognized and protected. She needed Carville's cooperation because the developer of the property would have to sign off on any suggestions regarding a memorial at Noor's burial site.

A long path from the office and barns curves gently down to the right, crossing Wolf Creek before emerging from a grove of trees near the west end of the training track. Dr. Peek and the others walked across the track into the infield, where the veterinarian tried to orient himself after more than thirty years.

"Remember, it's been a long time," he said.

Dr. Peek finally settled on an area almost directly across from the gate where the path from the barns met the outside rail of the track. Noor was buried in "this vicinity," he said, probably within a twenty-foot radius of where he was standing. It wasn't an exact location, and there was nothing obvious about the ground suggesting Dr. Peek's memory was accurate, but he seemed certain. And there was no one to contradict him.

It was a start.

Not a lot happened for more than a year.

Farmer continued to delve into Noor's history and lobbied Nell Scannon for a memorial of some kind to the horse. A newspaper article indicated that the Carville Sierra development plan for Loma Rica would include a horse park open to the public, with "a solar-powered, 60-stall public boarding facility, large indoor arena, outdoor arenas and roundpens, restored half-mile training track, acres of turnout pastures and miles of trails."[153] That sounded promising. Scannon seemed receptive to the idea for some sort of permanent memorial to Noor, and a tentative location for a statue was proposed.

Then everything changed.

By the start of 2010, a new developer was on board, and a revised plan for Loma Rica was under consideration by the Grass Valley Planning Commission. There were indications that the training track might not be retained in the new plan, and the status of Noor's grave suddenly was in question.

Farmer had to start over, with a new group of people to educate about Noor and the need to preserve his grave site.

On January 19, 2010, she braved a severe storm to meet with Thomas Last, planning director for the Grass Valley Community Development Department. During that meeting, she learned, among other things, that the forty-five-day period for comments on the Draft Environmental Impact Report (EIR) for the revised development plan would begin in a few weeks.

More troublesome was Last's suggestion that Noor was an issue with no historical significance, at least not at that point. He suggested that she pursue the matter during the later Design Phase of the Draft EIR:

> He finally got around to saying that since no one knew where *Noor was buried, what would be the purpose?
>
> To his surprise, I informed him that the general location of the grave, within a twenty-foot radius, had been identified thanks to Dr. Jon Peek, and if need be I could bring in Ground Penetrating Radar (GPR) to pinpoint the exact location. The tone of the meeting began to change. After that piece of information, he started to open up with suggestions on how I might protect *Noor. He said that knowing the general vicinity of the grave would be helpful, especially to Castle Construction, in furthering *Noor's cause.
>
> Also, the city council could condition the grave to be set aside and/or text could be added to protect the grave using Wolf Creek. Wolf Creek runs parallel to the training track on the north side. It is an environmentally sensitive area, and the setbacks that protect it could be extended out to encompass the grave. He said that the city council had the power to override the developer in this matter, and that might be an avenue to consider.

Steve Garrett was the new developer and spokesman for the Ronald Getty Trust, which owns the Loma Rica property. The Getty Trust purchased the Loma Rica property in 2002 and initially hired Carville Sierra as the local developer. The original proposal eschewed typical sprawling development in favor of a more environmentally friendly scheme that included some three hundred acres of open space, seven hundred residences of various sizes and a mix of commercial businesses. The concept was dubbed "new urbanism."[154]

Armed with a bundle of information about Noor, Farmer arranged a meeting with Steve Garrett in mid-February at Loma Rica. Garrett was an unknown, Farmer said, and she asked Rocky Freitas to accompany her to the meeting to answer any questions about the property. "I wanted to make sure I had my bases covered, as much as I could," she said.

> There was a light drizzle, so we waited inside the gazebo there at the ranch. Steve arrived in a black SUV, and when he got out, I thought, "You look like Bob Baffert, except your hair is dark."
>
> We introduced ourselves, and I handed him materials I had prepared giving him background on *Noor and the importance of protecting his grave. I mentioned that not only was he a Charles "Seabiscuit" Howard horse, who beat the great Citation, but he was of royal breeding, his first owner being His Highness the Aga Khan III. Steve gave no indication what he was thinking as I proceeded to talk about *Noor.
>
> Finally, he said he wanted to see the location.
>
> We got in our respective vehicles and drove out to the training track. Once there, I showed him the location of the grave where Dr. Peck said *Noor was buried. After seeing the location, he felt that the grave wouldn't be a problem given that *Noor was on the northeast corner of the track and the newly proposed Business Park would be constructed along the entire west side of the track.
>
> He asked me to walk with him, away from the others.
>
> It was then that he asked what it was that I wanted, and I said, "I want that grave," pointing in the direction of *Noor's grave. I further stated I wanted something in writing protecting the grave and filed with the city making it a matter of record.

Burley Parke and Noor on the backstretch. *Courtesy of the Parke family.*

He said that might be possible and he would be getting back in touch with me in a couple of weeks.

Farmer understood that Dr. Peek's best guess about the general area in the infield where Noor was buried wasn't going to be good enough, not if she wanted to be an effective advocate for Noor. She'd suggested the possibility of using ground-penetrating radar (GPR) to pinpoint the burial site when she met with the planning director, without actually knowing whether the equipment, or someone to operate it, was even available. Now she started looking in earnest.

She came across the name of Tom Nicholson, who lives in Grass Valley and who had the necessary GPR gear. He was intrigued by Farmer's story of Noor, and he had a connection with Loma Rica through his admiration for Errol MacBoyle.

A legend around Grass Valley, MacBoyle was a gold miner who made his fortune by ignoring supposed experts and by carrying on in the face of long odds. In that regard, MacBoyle was a lot like Charlotte Farmer, and maybe those were qualities that struck a chord with Nicholson. In any event, Nicholson volunteered his time and expertise for the search.

Early in the twentieth century, MacBoyle was associated with the Idaho-Maryland mine, a potentially rich producer of gold that wasn't making a profit for East Coast owner Harry Payne Whitney. MacBoyle didn't believe the geologists who said that a major fault rendered future mining efforts pointless. Instead, he obtained a lease with an option to buy from Whitney, scraped together enough money to purchase the property and reopened the mine.

Trying to revive an apparently exhausted gold mine was a long shot at best, but the gamble paid off.

The rich vein was relocated, and a reported $30 million in gold was mined during the next fifteen years. After a break in production during World War II, the mine reopened and stayed in business until the mid-1950s. Thanks largely to MacBoyle's perseverance, and a lot of luck along the way, the Idaho-Maryland mine eventually became the second-largest producer of gold in California.[155] With almost unlimited resources, MacBoyle started construction of Loma Rica in 1933.[156]

Farmer, Nicholson, Steve Garrett and a few others met at Loma Rica on the morning of March 16, 2010, for a try at pinpointing the exact location of Noor's grave. A ground-penetrating radar unit looks a lot like a cumbersome push mower, and Nicholson made sweep after sweep across the area identified by Dr. Peek. He was looking for patterns in the reflected waves indicating that "something" was buried under the ground. Ground-penetrating radar almost never produces distinct images, and interpreting the patterns is as much art as science.

> Leading up to this day, I had contacted trainer John Shirreffs. John had worked at Loma Rica for ten years under Henry Freitas and was there during *Noor's time. I asked him what he knew about the day *Noor died and how he might have been buried. He said he had been away from the ranch the day *Noor was put down and that Henry always had the horses facing the barn when he put them down...Once they were euthanized, they were "folded" into the grave. In *Noor's case, the grave would have been dug in a north-south fashion. *Noor would have been buried whole, no box, and no lime was used to help decompose the body.

*After about two hours of sweeping the area where Dr. Peek said *Noor was buried, and expanding out for about twenty feet, Tom kept coming back to one particular spot. It kept showing a ground anomaly of about five feet wide and eight feet long in the north-south direction John Shirreffs had said.*

It fit!

There were no other disturbances in the general vicinity. Tom left nothing to chance and continued to branch out from that spot, going over and over the area. Finally, he concluded that he had located the grave. One final act to perform, he plunged a long metal rod, which looked like rebar, into the ground. It cut through the ground with ease, indicating that something was buried there.

There was no doubt the grave had been located.

Afterward, Steve and I talked as we walked away from the others. Again, he asked what it was that I wanted. Once again, I pointed to the grave and said, "I want that grave."

He said something could be worked out, but it would have to wait until <u>after</u> everything was through the process. I told him that didn't work for me; I wanted something in writing, on file with the city, or I would continue my quest to protect the grave.

That is where we left it.

The idea of exhuming Noor's remains and moving them somewhere else hadn't entered anyone's mind yet, for a couple of very good reasons. First, there still was hope that the grave would be protected in the development plans for Loma Rica. Maybe more important, locating the horse's grave and then convincing the Grass Valley Planning Commission to protect the site was a daunting enough idea; locating the grave, disinterring Noor, working out a substitute burial site, transporting and reburying the remains—that was something else entirely.

Steve Garrett and the Getty Trust were being cooperative, but by September it was becoming clear that protecting Noor's grave site wasn't particularly high on the priority list of any of the decision makers. Farmer was beginning to think that Noor never would receive the appreciation and respect he deserved and that the grave site couldn't be protected from future development in Grass Valley:

With that in mind, I needed to find out everything I could about exhuming the remains of a horse, especially one that had been dead for thirty-six years. I decided to see what information was available regarding Man o' War's removal from Faraway Farm to the Kentucky Horse Park.

I contacted the Horse Park and was put through to Bill Cooke, director of the Horse Park's International Museum of the Horse. I told Bill about *Noor and the possible plans to move him, and I needed to know what to expect. Maybe I might find some useful information in articles surrounding the removal of Man o' War. Bill was very gracious and said he would look into it and see what they might have on hand and get back in touch with me.

He discovered that they have quite a file on the 1976 removal of Man o' War's remains, and he would send me copies of the material. He noticed, while reading through the articles, that it mentioned David Hager Sr. as the person who had been in charge of the dig. His suggestion was that I should check and see if he was still alive and talk with him.

Once I received the materials, and with that information in hand, I started looking for a David Hager Sr. in the Lexington area.

I got lucky and obtained a phone number. I called and introduced myself. I told David my story and that, at some point, I planned to dig *Noor up and move him out of Grass Valley. We must have talked for over two hours. He filled me in on the in-and-outs of digging up horses and what to expect. Man o' War, War Relic and War Admiral had not been dead as long as *Noor, plus Man o' War had been embalmed. Four hundred pounds of bones had been recovered from Man o' War's grave.

Wow!

As we talked, I made note of things that I needed to be cautious about: need to be careful about the equipment don't use a backhoe with teeth, as it would tear into the grave and disturb the remains; the bones will be very fragile, if I found any; and if the dig lasted beyond one day, make sure to post a guard to keep souvenir hunters away. I found the information very informative.

> He said he has film of the excavation, along with pictures, and went into great detail about the embalming of Man o' War. It was his funeral home that had facilitated the embalming of Big Red. In some ways, I learned more than I wished to regarding that.

In early September, Farmer attended another in what must have seemed like an endless succession of planning meetings in Grass Valley. It was a Joint Study Session of the planning commission and the city council, an important meeting that Farmer likened to the D-Day invasion. There would be an opportunity for public comments, which was why Farmer was there, but there was a complication—each speaker would be limited to only three minutes.

Farmer can talk about Noor for hours; sometimes it takes her three minutes just to say "hello."

> The meeting was called to order and eventually was opened up for public comment. I made sure I was the first one up.
> Three minutes, that's all I had.
> There were three lights on the podium, green, yellow and red. When the yellow light comes on, you had better be winding up what you are saying.
> I identified myself and reminded them that I had spoken before them back on March 16 about locating *Noor's grave. I stated that I had prepared packets for each of them, along with their respective clerks, and a counter copy for each department. Within the packets they would find the necessary information on *Noor with which to make a decision, hopefully, in favor of protecting the grave.
> I mentioned that it had come to my attention that *Noor was being referenced as "just a horse." I said that "he was not just a horse as Chuck Yeager is not just a pilot." Chuck Yeager lives in the area and as everyone knew was one of the most famous test pilots of all time, having traveled faster than the speed of sound in 1947.
> I also brought it to their attention that I had learned that there were those who were saying that the grave was not that of *Noor. That is when I produced the letter from Rocky stating that, yes, indeed that is where *Noor's grave was

> and that Dr. Peek had originally identified the location...In conclusion, I once again asked that:
> *Noor be recognized, by this body, as a horse of historic value and as such be shown the respect that a champion of his caliber deserves by protecting his grave, and that, should at some point in the future the occasion arise to move his remains out of California, it be part of the conditions protecting the grave.
> You could have heard a pin drop when I mentioned number two. I thanked them and took my seat.

In the months to come, the concern about future plans for Noor's grave would prove to be well founded.

In February 2011, the Grass Valley Planning Commission voted five to zero to approve an environmental review for the Loma Rica development. The review did not specifically discuss the grave site of Noor as a historic or cultural resource and apparently wasn't required to do so under state law. The plans for a horse park had been scrapped and replaced by a commercial area that would include the training track.[157]

The Loma Rica Ranch Specific Plan approved a few months later confirmed the change in plans: "The horse track...will not be retained as a horse track. It will be developed as part of the business park. Its proximity to Wolf Creek and the open space will provide a pleasing environment for the people who work in the business park."[158]

The May 2011 Specific Plan did include a provision for "6,000 to 8,000 square feet of land for a memorial site to recognize the historical value of the horse Noor,"[159] but with development of the planned business park, it was clear that the memorial would be somewhere other than the actual place where Noor was buried.

If there was a watershed moment for Farmer, it came in early November 2010.

The decision to find another burial site for Noor had been made, but there were innumerable hurdles to overcome—technical problems associated with exhuming a horse and transporting the remains, finding a new burial site and raising money among them. First, though, there were a couple pressing legal issues to address. They arose because Farmer was an interested party with no legal right to do much of anything.

First was access to the burial site. Loma Rica was private property belonging to someone else, and Farmer would have to obtain permission to dig there. And then there was the question of who actually owned Noor's remains. It was easy to trace Noor's ownership while the horse was alive, from the Aga Khan, who bred him; to Charles Howard, who bought him; to the estate, which took over after Howard's death. But did anyone have an ownership interest in Noor's remains some four decades after the horse's death? If so, who? Had the remains been abandoned, or did ownership pass to the Getty Trust when Loma Rica's current owners bought the property?

These questions became moot thanks to a contract between Steve Garrett and Kittredge ("Kit") Collins. Garrett was acting on behalf of the Getty Trust, and he gave permission for the exhumation; Kit Collins is a great-grandson of Charles Howard, and he approved.

There was a condition, though. Timing was an issue due to the pending development plans for Loma Rica, and the agreement gave Farmer only eighteen months, until mid-May 2012, to move Noor's remains. Considering that the ground would be too wet for excavation for most of the winter, eighteen months wasn't very much time.

Farmer contacted the Kentucky Horse Park near Lexington for permission to move Noor's remains there, but that apparently wouldn't work. Executive director John Nicholson explained that burial there was reserved for horses that lived and died at the horse park. There was a possible loophole for extenuating circumstances particular to a specific horse, but Noor didn't seem to qualify.

Nicholson suggested that Farmer get in touch with the tracks in California where Noor had raced with such distinction. If Noor could not be buried at those tracks, that might be a justification—an extenuating circumstance—for the Horse Park Board of Directors to allow Noor's burial.

It sounded like a good idea. Noor had been a star up and down the California coast, and finding a racetrack that would welcome his remains with open arms should have been easy.

It wasn't.

Hollywood Park was out of the running because at the time the future of the facility was in question. The track site had been sold a couple of times, it was approved for large-scale commercial development and there were rumors than it would close.[160] Early in 2012, close to the contractual deadline for moving Noor's remains, the Hollywood Park Racing Association

Joyce Brainard carried the Hollywood Gold Cup to Noor's stall for the horse's inspection. *Courtesy of the Parke family.*

and Betfair U.S. entered into an agreement that will keep the track open for at least another five years as Betfair Hollywood Park.[161]

Officials at Golden Gate Fields in Northern California declined Farmer's offer, saying that the infield at the track was considered an environmentally sensitive wetland. The paddock area at Santa Anita was not an option, but there was no decision about a burial somewhere else at the track. Farmer knew that a move to the National Museum of Racing in Saratoga, New York, was a longshot, but a longshot was starting to look like the best bet available. Zoning issues thwarted that option, however.

Winter turned into spring. Farmer and Kit Collins were becoming increasingly frustrated at the chilly receptions they were getting from people whom they thought would have been interested in providing a final resting place for Noor.

"This was a Hall of Fame horse, not some nag we were trying to palm off on someone," Farmer said of the failed efforts.

Old Friends

While Farmer was trying to negotiate the official channels and running up against one stone wall after another, a grassroots campaign in support of Noor was growing on Facebook, mainly through a very popular website set up to honor Horse of the Year Zenyatta.[162] In an April 28, 2011 posting to the website, Farmer mentioned Noor and the horse's connection to trainer John Shirreffs, who also trained Zenyatta. The response was overwhelming and unexpected.

Two months later, word of Farmer's campaign to find a new resting place for Noor's remains was attracting a lot of traffic at the Zenyatta website. She was starting to get some national press attention, too, which was a far cry from the local media in Grass Valley that had largely ignored her efforts until *after* an article appeared in the *Los Angeles Times*. Donations weren't pouring in, not exactly, but money was coming at a regular clip.

Most important of all, a white knight had materialized for Farmer and Noor in the person of Michael Blowen, a retired *Boston Globe* journalist who owns Old Friends outside Georgetown, Kentucky. Old Friends is a retirement farm for Thoroughbreds, and Blowen thought the farm would be the perfect spot for Noor. On June 15, he shared the news on the Zenyatta Facebook page:

> We are very excited that Charlotte and Kit have chosen Old Friends as the final resting place for that great Hall-of-Famer, Noor... We are working with The National Hall of Fame in Saratoga Springs on a program to ensure that all these late, great athletes have an appropriate place where their fans can pay their respects. We're very grateful to everyone for allowing us to be that place. If everything works out, Noor should be relocated to Old Friends in Georgetown, Ky. in August.

The pieces of the puzzle finally were starting to fall into place.

Erin Dwyer, an archaeologist working for the California Department of Transportation and a horse lover, joined the team, and there was sufficient money to defray the cost of a special box to transport Noor's remains.

> Enough donation money had come in by this time so that Michael Blowen was able to send me the needed monies to begin construction of the box that would hold Noor's remains. The box would be eight feet long by four feet wide by four feet deep and made of birch hardwood plywood. I chose a

stain called "Driftwood," and a polyurethane clear satin to go over it. It would be lined with a plastic twelve-mil polycarbonate sheeting cloudy/clear. The lid would have C.S. Howard's red and white Triangle H logo emblazoned on it, along with a nameplate that I had bought for *Noor.

It would take Willie nearly five weeks to complete the box.

The exhumation of Noor was scheduled for August 26. A month before that, a second ground-penetrating radar sweep of the infield apparently had confirmed the location of Noor's burial site.

While Tom was working the GPR, Erin went around looking at the ground and periodically scraping dirt. I finally asked her what she was doing. She said that she was looking for gopher mounds. It seems that gophers have been known to bring up bone fragments, which mixes in with the dirt. The test as to whether it is bone pieces, and I am talking very small—less than the size of an eraser head on a pencil, is you put the piece on your tongue, and if it sticks it is bone.

So far, no bones.

She found a marker that was in the ground, near the grave, and identified it as being from the late 1960s/early 1970s. Timeline was right; Noor died in 1974. We came to the conclusion that Henry Freitas must have put it there as a marker.

I had concerns that after thirty-six years there would be nothing left of him other than dark, rich dirt. Erin assured me we would find remains and explained, as an archaeologist, that the ground and the climate were all positive for preservation. She had been on digs that yielded skeletal remains of indigenous Native Americans that had been in the ground far longer than *Noor. I was not to worry.

Tom showed Erin the ground anomaly as it appeared on his equipment. It was in the same place as before. It only took an hour. Once again, he took the rebar-looking rod and drove it into the ground, only this time it didn't go down; the ground was so dry.

With that, we were done.

Once again, *Noor's location had been confirmed.

Old Friends

The exhumation of Noor's remains at Loma Rica began badly. The owner of the backhoe substituted a bucket with teeth for the smooth-edged bucket Farmer had requested. David Hager Sr., who supervised the exhumation of Man o' War, had advised Farmer that a bucket with teeth could destroy the remains, and Erin Dwyer agreed that a grading bucket was a safer choice. The ground was too hard for a smooth-edged blade, the backhoe owner explained, and digging began at the location indicated by the ground-penetrating radar.

> The backhoe starts bringing up thick, dark, rich dirt—we have him!
> Erin examines it and says it is not *Noor.
> The backhoe continues digging deeper.
> Rocky arrives, followed by Dr. Peek. I stay away from the dig, observing from a distance. For whatever reason, I just don't want to be close as they dig. Anyway, I have enough eyes watching for me, especially Erin's. They have now gone down twelve feet, but no *Noor. The backhoe continues to bring up thick, dark, rich dirt, so we must have *Noor.
> "No, we don't," as Erin explains, it is swamp fill, which possibly was used to cover a swampy area on the track long ago.
> The backhoe begins widening the area of the dig; still no *Noor. Where is he?
> I go over to where Erin and Denise are standing, asking them, "Why can't this dirt be *Noor? It looks exactly like what I was told we would find, dark and thick in texture." Yes, I realize they are the experts and have said this is swamp fill, but my mind keeps saying, "Why isn't this dirt *Noor?"
> It is not looking good. Burley Parke's granddaughter and husband arrive from Santa Rosa, as do Kittredge (Kit) and his wife, Suzie. I break the news to them that *Noor is not where we thought he was. The air has now taken on a somber tone.
> The mound of dirt gets higher and higher as the backhoe continues to widen its search looking for *Noor. The hole is now thirteen feet deep and thirty feet wide. The black soil is

everywhere, once again confirming Erin's theory—this is fill. His grave is not where the GPR indicated, nor where Dr. Peek remembered it as being.

It is surreal.

As I look around, Dr. Peek is on the west end of the track talking to someone; Willie, Erin, Denise, Kit, Rocky, Eldon and Gary are out by the hole. The noise of the backhoe blocks the deafening quiet of thoughts.

I go over to where Dr. Peek is standing. He informs me that he has to leave, but he is confident we will find *Noor. He is excited. I am very unhappy at the thoughts of him leaving because Dr. Peek is my rock, the only living person who was there the day *Noor was put down, and now he has to leave. I stand there and stare at what is happening there in the infield of the training track and feel sick.

The morning seems to go on forever... The backhoe keeps digging, and the mound of dirt keeps growing. It is now around ten feet tall.

I can't sit.

Where is he?

Everyone keeps telling me to get out of the sun and sit down. Eldon and Gary have set up their cameras on tripods, filming the backhoe as it goes about its work... I just watch and keep hoping, he has to be somewhere in that area.

It is starting to get hot. It is now around 11:00 a.m., only 11:00 a.m.... Kit and I look grim, still no *Noor. Suzie tells me that she told Kit he didn't have to come, but he insisted on being here. Gary tries to keep my spirits up by tapping under his chin, motioning chin up, and Eldon keeps smiling. All that does is bring tears to my eyes, and at one point I start to cry. Rocky comforts me, saying we will find him, just have faith. Erin assures me, with such confidence, that we will find him.

Erin Dwyer is a principal investigator of prehistoric archaeology for the California Department of Transportation. She works mainly as a supervisor, dealing with myriad oversight and regulatory issues that crop up while negotiating the maze of state and federal laws that protect Native American and other historical sites. She'd paid her dues in the field, though, and the dig at Loma Rica was a welcome diversion from her desk

Old Friends

Archaeologist Erin Dwyer sifting for bone fragments at Loma Rica Ranch. *Courtesy of Denise Jaffke.*

job. It didn't hurt that horse racing is her passion, which made her a good fit with Farmer.

She had offered to help with the excavation after reading an article about Farmer and Noor in the *Los Angeles Times*, and Farmer quickly accepted. Dwyer later would say that it turned out to be the most stressful day of her life.

Dwyer's colleague at Loma Rica that day was a friend, Denise Jaffke. Like Dwyer, she has a day job, field work at high altitude sites as associate state archaeologist for the California Department of Parks and Recreation. Unlike Erin, who breeds and races Thoroughbreds on a small scale, Denise didn't come to Loma Rica with an equine background. She wasn't even sure what role she'd play, beyond serving as another pair of trained eyes.

She also didn't realize the scope of the project, the number of people involved or the emotions.

By mid-morning, both Dwyer and Jaffke began to doubt that they were digging in the right place. The ground-penetrating radar said that they were, but their eyes and their experience told them otherwise.

"The backhoe kept going deeper and deeper," Dwyer recalled. "We got ten feet down, and I thought that was too deep. They wouldn't have done that in the 1970s. When we first hit a dark layer, an organic layer, we thought it was Noor, but we got nothing. We found some grass that had been preserved, but no bones. They'd filled in a swamp to level the track, and that must have been the source of the organic material.

"We started expanding the hole, but we still got nothing. The area we had opened up was staggering."

The problem, Dwyer was beginning to think, was the ground-penetrating radar. The equipment was getting better and better, but it wasn't perfect. Even a skilled operator got hits and misses, and many of the hits were false. The device had picked up an anomaly in the earth where they were digging, but the archaeologists now were certain that it wasn't the burial site. But if not, where was Noor? The only clues had been the ground-penetrating radar and Dr. Peek's memory, and both apparently had pointed them in the wrong direction.

By lunchtime, everyone was hot, tired and discouraged. Although there still was a half day to work, the possibility that Noor's remains wouldn't be found was real. The question that no one was ready to ask was whether the exhumation and reburial would have to be a symbolic one, without the actual recovery of any of Noor's bones.

During the lunch break, Gary Parke and his brother, Eldon, began mulling over an idea. Henry Freitas had been a man like their father, Burley, they thought, someone with a deep respect for the horses in his care. They didn't believe that selecting the burial site for a champion like Noor would have been a haphazard choice, and they tried to visualize Freitas's thinking as he picked a location.

They used a laser rangefinder to locate a point exactly equidistant from three reference points—the inner rail of the training track midway around the turn and points where the long straightaways both entered and exited the turn. Think of the turn as one half of a full circle, and the point they came up with would be the center. Dwyer agreed that the new location was promising:

Rocky tells them her father had told her that *Noor was buried near the white box, which is still there in the infield. Gary and Eldon add the possibility Henry would have mentally drawn lines, east-west and north-south; using the center part of the west end of the track's fence bringing the line down to where it would intersect with the imaginary line running east-west—lining up with the box.

The backhoe begins digging in this new location.

The first few scoops of dirt turned up the bone Gary Parke found. At six feet, they found the first long bone. Dwyer was certain that they had uncovered Noor's burial site.

"It was him," she said. "It had to be, a no-brainer. But we weren't absolutely sure until we found the first horseshoe. Noor's shoes weren't very big."

> They continue to find bones and even two of *Noor's horseshoes. At some point, someone puts one of *Noor's horseshoes into my hand. I hold onto it, noticing that it is heavy with a thick crust all over it. Finally, I slip it over the arm of one of the chairs. I have no desire to look at the bones. This is *Noor, and other than Erin or Denise, it doesn't seem right for everyone to be handling him. I know they all are helping...

Jaffke climbed into the bucket of the backhoe and had the operator lower her into the hole. She wanted to examine the walls of the trench, looking for a subtle change in the color or composition of the soil. She needed to see a boundary layer, something more organic, something darker, so she could direct the backhoe operator. Discovery of a similar dark layer during the morning excavation at the original site had raised false hopes. Now that the first bones had been found, everyone knew that they had found Noor's grave.

Loading Noor's remains for the drive to Old Friends. *Courtesy of Denise Jaffke.*

The skeleton was not intact, and the condition of the bones surprised Dwyer and Jaffke.

"The remains were very fragmentary," Dwyer recalled. "I expected them to be in better condition because this was not an old burial site by our standards. I've found very old sites that were in better shape."

Archaeologists have a particular way of doing things to preserve the integrity of an excavation. Discovery of a burial site like this one ordinarily would have been the first step in a lengthy process—careful digging with hand tools, sifting the soil through wire screens for tiny relics, cataloguing and photographing. But there was no time.

"We wanted to be particular, but we didn't have time," Dwyer said. "I wish we could have done it in a more respectful way, more sensitive. Instead, all they had time to do was load the truck."

> Willie stands by the side of the pickup as Travis continues to fill the box with *Noor's remains. Because of the teeth on the bucket, we are scooping up a lot of dirt with the remains. With all the dirt and *Noor mixed together we have about three tons. By this time the pickup cannot handle any more, and Willie tells Travis to stop. Travis takes the remaining dirt and spreads it out over the ground.
>
> Erin begins going through it, checking to see if anything has been overlooked. Denise goes back down into the hole, making sure that nothing has been missed. If there was more time, Erin could use her screens to sift through the remaining dirt, but the backhoe has to be back in the yard before 4:30 p.m., and the hole still needs to be filled in.
>
> Eldon and Gary take Global Positioning System coordinates of the grave. That way the grave won't be lost for a <u>second time</u>. You never know, maybe at some point in the future a marker could be placed on the grave.
>
> Willie motions for me to come over to the pickup. He asks me how I want things arranged in the box.
>
> I tell him I want the bones laid on top of the dirt along with the letters and the dirt from the three racetracks. I make sure the horseshoe that I had been handed goes into the box with *Noor. Everything that went into the ground with *Noor in 1974, bones and horseshoes, are now with him in the box.

Robin McHargue provided dirt from the Golden Gate Fields winner's circle. *Courtesy of Ariadana Scott.*

I had given a select few the opportunity to put something in the box with *Noor. My instructions were that it could be no larger than a legal size envelope, and whatever they sent to me, I would not open; it would stay between *Noor and each one of them.

Once I received their letters, I had them sealed in plastic, including mine. I already had dirt from the winner's circle of Hollywood Park and Santa Anita, thanks to my friends Kip and Vivian, and Ariadne had gotten dirt from Golden Gate Fields. It was symbolic, but I wanted soil from the winner's circle of the three tracks where he achieved his greatest victories, two being against the great Citation, to be with him always.

Rocky offered Loma Rica's original saddlecloths for *Noor. She had sewn together three of the saddlecloths, which was laid over him. Everything was arranged, and Gary, Eldon and Kit help Willie put the lid on the box. The box has shifted due to the loading of *Noor, so the screw holes are not lining up. Finally, they are able to line up the holes and put the screws in.

The boy is secure, and he now belongs to me!

10
Old Friends

It's difficult to believe in guardian angels these days, especially with so much wrong in the world. If anybody can claim one, though, it might be Charlotte Farmer. She's convinced that the spirit of a handsome black horse, head held high like his sire Nasrullah, with a little white on his forehead and one white ankle, watched over her throughout the cross-country journey from Loma Rica to Kentucky.

She might be right.

It was a brutal trip, packed with twelve-hour driving days and generic courtesy breakfasts at cookie-cutter motels—Grass Valley to Reno on Friday; to Salt Lake City on Saturday; to Oakley, Kansas, on Sunday; to Mt. Vernon, Illinois, on Monday; to Georgetown, Kentucky, on Tuesday—more than 2,200 miles, all spent in a huge Dodge Ram 3500 diesel with dual wheels and a long bed to carry the box holding Noor's remains. All sorts of things could have gone wrong but didn't. No accidents, no mechanical problems, no vandals poking around under the tarp that covered the wooden box. Even a chance encounter with a state trooper in Kansas turned out all right.

> *Willie needs to get diesel and pulls behind a big rig. A state trooper is close by. Yep, we get pulled over. State trooper informs Willie he is traveling too close to the big rig.*
>
> *Willie explains that he was getting ready to pull off at the next exit to get diesel. The story doesn't fly with the trooper. I give him our registration, and he asks, "What's in the box?"*

Charlotte Farmer: "Without her, none of this would have happened." *Courtesy of the author.*

> I say, "A dead horse!"
> He looks rather startled. I ask him, "Please tell me you have heard of Charles 'Seabiscuit' Howard?"
> He has.
> "Well, this is his other champion, *Noor." I explain that we have dug *Noor up and are in the process of transporting him back to Old Friends in Georgetown, Kentucky, to be buried and the reasons why.
> He comments that the boys back at the station are not going to believe this one. He lets us go with a warning to Willie to stay off the back bumpers of vehicles and says we will find diesel at the next exit.
> Drive safe!

The guardian angel at work again!

The dedication ceremony for Noor's grave took place on Wednesday, August 31, in a small, fenced paddock adjacent to the office at Old Friends. It was another hot summer day, but one without the tension and urgency that had accompanied the exhumation a few days earlier at Loma Rica. There was sadness, certainly, but there also was an almost palpable sense of relief that Noor's final journey had come to an end in the most appropriate place imaginable.

"Today we're paying respect to one of the greatest racehorses ever," Old Friends owner Michael Blowen said. It wasn't an exaggeration, although it probably came as a surprise to the visitors who were unfamiliar with Noor's accomplishments.

Charlotte and Willie were there, of course. So was Burley Parke's son, Gary, who flew in from Utah for the ceremony; a few reporters and photographers; a fan of Noor who brought a stack of old magazines recounting Noor's exploits on the track; supporters of Old Friends; local horse enthusiasts; and a smattering of people who were simply curious about all the commotion.

Bucky Sallee, longtime bugler at Keeneland racetrack a few miles down the road in Lexington, blew a final Call to the Post.

Burley Parke's son, Gary, at Old Friends. *Courtesy of the author.*

A few toasts to Noor and then it was over. The bottle of Woodford Reserve bourbon was placed with other bottles from special occasions at Old Friends.

One of the large red roses has broken off, and I pick it up and place it behind the headstone underneath my words. People are slowly leaving. Even though it is still morning, I pour a shot of Woodford and go over to *Noor's grave and toast him. Finally, I am by myself. I see Willie coming over, but he turns around and leaves me to my thoughts. I lean over and kiss the headstone and tell the big boy I love him.

Old Friends

Old Friends owner Michael Blowen. *Courtesy of the author.*

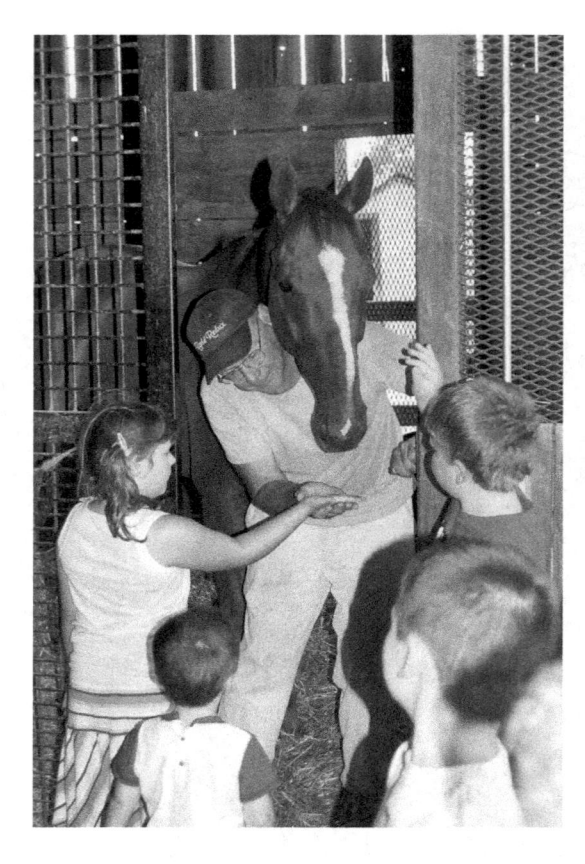

Michael Blowen, twenty-two-race winner Rapid Redux and visitors to Old Friends. *Courtesy of the author.*

Old Friends is such a logical site for the memorial to a champion like Noor that now, after the fact, it's a wonder that no one thought of it sooner. The retirement home for almost one hundred Thoroughbreds in Kentucky and another dozen at a farm near Saratoga in New York, with collective earnings on the track of more than $90 million, Old Friends is the brainchild of owner Michael Blowen. He's a retiree himself from the *Boston Globe*, and his story is as unlikely as Farmer's campaign on behalf of Noor.[163]

Although Blowen doesn't have a background in racing, he has become one of the sport's most effective ambassadors. Visitors flock to Old Friends, fifteen to seventeen thousand people every year, and Blowen works the crowds with an enthusiasm that is contagious. He knows the racing history of each of the farm's residents, and maybe more importantly, he knows their quirks and idiosyncrasies, the little things that visitors will remember. He's a fan and an advocate when racing needs both.

Blowen wrote movie reviews and travel pieces for the *Globe* and occasionally went to the track with an editor friend, Robert Taylor. He liked the gambling more than he liked the horses, and one day it occurred to him that he might be a better handicapper if he knew a little more about the animals he was betting on. Blowen knew a small-time trainer, Carlos Figueroa (known as the "King of the Fairs" in Massachusetts), and he offered to work as a groom in return for some schooling.

Not one to turn down free help, Figueroa said yes. Blowen worked on the backstretch in the early morning for two years while he kept his day job at the *Globe*. He called it his "secret identity."

"I fell in love with the horses," Blowen recalled. "I loved to be around them. But the slaughter trucks were coming and going all the time, and I decided I wanted to do something for the horses if I could."

A trip to the Kentucky Horse Park outside Lexington for a travel article sealed the deal.

"I loved the Horse Park," he said. "I wrote a lot of movie reviews for the paper, but I never was star struck by the actors. But I was star struck by the horses."

Blowen retired from the *Globe* with a decent severance package after the *New York Times* bought the paper in 1993 and started looking around for something else to occupy his time. He worked for a while as the operations director for the Thoroughbred Retirement Foundation, a job that required a move to Kentucky.

"My wife [popular *Globe* columnist Diane White] said she would move to Kentucky on one condition," Blowen said. "If she decided to leave home, I had to promise not to look for her."

The TRF job lasted about a year and a half, with Blowen chomping at the bit to open his own retirement farm all the while. When that happened, he had two goals for Old Friends, both of them unconventional.

"I didn't want to duplicate what the other retirement farms were doing," Blowen explained. "Retired stallions needed a place, and we decided to take stallions when no one else was doing that." Other farms were turning stallions away because they can be more difficult to handle than mares and geldings. Blowen wanted to attract visitors to the farm, and he realized that prominent stallions could be the "stars" that would attract people.

"I knew from covering the movies, stars are very important. If you don't have a star, you don't have a movie. So that was always in the back of my mind."

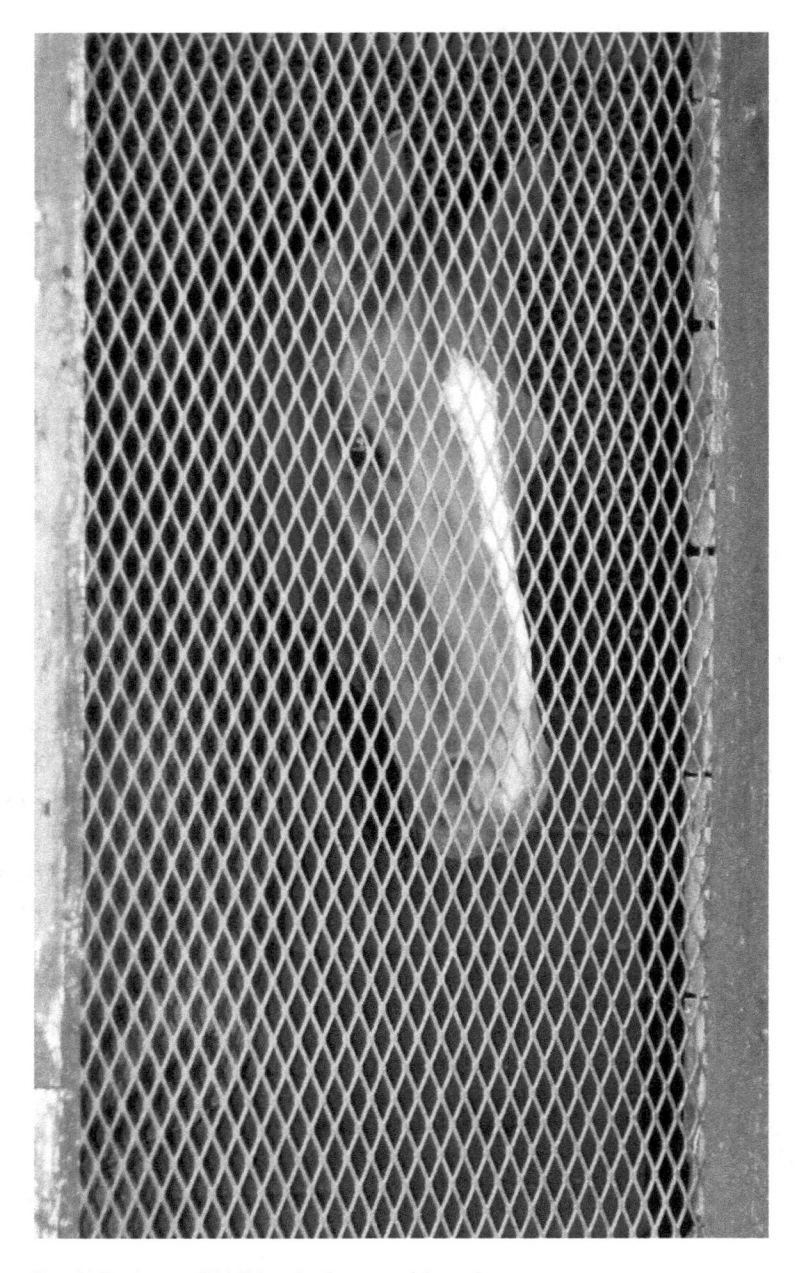

Rapid Redux at Old Friends. *Courtesy of the author.*

Blowen's star system also was a key element in his other goal for Old Friends, proving that the horses still could generate some income *after* they were through racing. Visiting Old Friends is free, but the gift store does a brisk business, and donations, large and small, keep coming in.

"If these horses can make some money in retirement, that would solve everything," he said. "It would be an incentive for other farms to give them a place to live."

Noor found a home at Old Friends through a mix of Charlotte Farmer's persistence and Michael Blowen's respect for unconventional thinking. "I got an e-mail from Charlotte sometime in the fall of 2010," Blowen said.

> *She talked about the development plans for Loma Rica and the fear that someone might pave over Noor's grave. She was looking for a place to move him. I've always been attracted to people who think outside the box. I don't want to say "no." I want to find a way to make things happen.*
>
> *I had no reservations about finding a place for Noor. I wanted him here, but at the time, I didn't think she could get it done. I thought that she'd eventually give up. But I couldn't have been more wrong.*

Noor's grave is marked, finally after almost forty years, with a gray headstone. One side has factual information summarizing Noor's pedigree, racing record, breeder, owner and trainer. The other side has a more personal message from Charlotte Farmer carved into the light gray stone:

NOOR

NOOR, A HORSE OF ROYAL BREEDING, NOW SLEEPS. HIS NAME ECHOES WITH SWEET WHISPERS DOWN THE LONG CORRIDORS OF RACING'S PAST. HIS WINNING SPIRIT NOW SHINES IN THE SUNLIGHT ONCE AGAIN, AS HE HOLDS COURT FOR ALL WHO COME TO SAY, "WELL DONE."

A marker memorializing Noor. *Courtesy of the author.*

A similar "well done" could be said of Farmer, who proved to be as much a guardian angel for Noor as the horse's indefatigable spirit was for her. Noor never quit trying as a racehorse and neither did she as his tireless advocate. In the end, after Noor's remains were laid to rest for the last time, Farmer could look back on two remarkable journeys—hers and Noor's—and smile.

NOTES

INTRODUCTION

1. An excellent account of Ben Hogan's injury, recovery and return to championship-level play can be found in chapters 13 and 14 of Dodson's *American Triumvirate*.
2. Hirsch and Plowden, *In the Winner's Circle*, 89.
3. Bowen, *Masters of the Turf*, 272.
4. Bill Christine, "Cigar Goes Got Special Citation Mark Today," *Los Angeles Times*, July 13, 1996.
5. Irish-bred Noor raced in this country as *Noor, the asterisk added by the Jockey Club indicating that he was bred in a foreign country and imported to the United States for racing or breeding. Asterisks were used for this designation from 1906 through 1974. Beginning in 1975, the asterisk for foreign-bred horses was dropped and replaced by a country-specific code following the horse's name—Noor (Ire), for example. Following the suggestion of Shannon Luce, communications coordinator for the Jockey Club, who indicated that Noor was a protected name and that neither an asterisk nor a country code was necessary, Noor's name without an asterisk will be used throughout this book. Asterisks appearing in direct quotes are retained.

6. Staff of the *Blood-Horse* magazine compiled several "best of" books during the last few years. The Noor-Citation series didn't receive a mention in *Horse Racing's Greatest Rivalries*, a puzzling omission. Noor was ranked sixty-ninth in *Thoroughbred Champions: Top 100 Racehorses of the 20th Century*. Citation, defeated by Noor four times, was third among the century's best horses, behind only Man o' War and Secretariat. In *Horse Racing's Top 100 Moments*, Citation merits two entries (as racing's first millionaire, No. 43, and for his sixteen-race winning streak, No. 67); Noor gets a mention, albeit indirectly and not even by name, in the book's entry (No. 23) regarding the importation to the United States of Nasrullah, Noor's sire.
7. Hirsch and Plowden, *In the Winner's Circle*, 169.

Chapter 1

8. *New York Times*, "Seabiscuit Dies of Heart Attack at C.S. Howard Ranch on Coast," May 19, 1947.
9. McEvoy, *Seabiscuit Story*, 93; "Seabiscuit Dies in California," *Blood-Horse* (May 24, 1947). The book was a compilation of articles about Seabiscuit that appeared in the *Blood-Horse* magazine from July 1935 through January 1982. References are made to the book and to the individual articles.
10. Hillenbrand, *Seabiscuit*, 339.
11. Ibid., 336–39.
12. McEvoy, *Seabiscuit Story*, 86; "Tourist Attraction," *Blood-Horse* (September 27, 2941).
13. *American Racing Manual*, 1941 edition (Triangle Publications).
14. McEvoy, *Seabiscuit Story*, 96–100; "Obituary of Charles Stuart Howard," *Blood-Horse* (June 10, 1950).
15. McEvoy, *Seabiscuit Story*, 95; "Seabiscuit Dies in California," *Blood-Horse* (May 24, 1947).
16. McEvoy, *Seabiscuit Story*, 117; Kent Hollingsworth, "Seabiscuit," *Blood-Horse* (April 18, 1970).
17. McEvoy, *Seabiscuit Story*, 97–98; "Obituary of Charles Stuart Howard," *Blood-Horse* (June 10, 1950).
18. *Horse Racing's Top 100 Moments* (Lexington, KY: Eclipse Press, 2006), 95. There is some discrepancy about how much it cost to syndicate Nasrullah. Other press reports put the price at $372,000. Paul Zimmerman, "Noor Defeats Citation in Stretch Drive," *Los Angeles Times*, February 26, 1950.

19. "Financial necessity" during World War II prompted the sale of some of the Aga Khan's best stallions. Jodidio, *Racing and Breeding Tradition*, 59–60.
20. Palmer, *American Race Horses*, 43.
21. *Horse Racing's Top 100 Moments*, 94–95.
22. The Curse of the Kohinoor Diamond says: "He who owns this diamond will own the world but also will know all its misfortunes. Only God, or a woman, can wear it with impunity." The diamond now is part of the British Crown Jewels. Since the reign of Queen Victoria, the Kohinoor has passed to the wife of the male heir to the British throne. http://www.diamonds-are-forever.org.uk/kohinoor-diamond.htm.
23. John P. Sparkman, "Montjeu and a Piece of Wood," *Thoroughbred Times*, July 7, 2012, 50.
24. Robert Hebert, "*Khaled, *Old English, and Some New Notes About *Noor," *Blood-Horse* (February 8, 1950).
25. Oscar Otis, "Foreign Stars Successful in Big 'Cap," *Daily Racing Form*, February 25, 1950.
26. "Obituary of Burley Parke," *Blood-Horse*, October 17, 1977, 4882–83. The purchase price for Nathoo and Noor was reported as $150,000 in the British *Bloodstock Breeders Review* for 1950.
27. *American Racing Manual*, 1951 edition, 59–62.
28. Ibid.

Chapter 2

29. "Obituary of Burley Parke," *Blood-Horse*, October 17, 1977, 4882–83.
30. "Firing," also the treatment of choice for Citation after the 1948 Tanforan Handicap, involves applying a hot iron or needles to an affected part of the leg in an effort to create inflammation and thereby increase blood flow to the area. The procedure is extremely painful for the horse, and there is scant evidence that it actually works. Consensus is that it is the enforced period of rest after firing that actually promotes healing of both the injury and the burns created by the firing iron. Landers, *Professional Care*, 223–23.
31. Oscar Otis, "Foreign Stars Successful in Big 'Cap," *Daily Racing Form*, February 25, 1950.
32. Hewitt, *Sire Lines*, 142.
33. "Obituary of Burley Parke," 4882–83.

34. Information about the Parke family was gathered from several sources, including contemporaneous accounts of Noor's 1949 and 1950 seasons; an obituary of Burley Parke, *Blood-Horse*, October 17, 1977, 4882–83; a *Daily Racing Form* interview by Oscar Otis, "Trainer Burley Parke Recalls His Early Days on Race Track," June 27, 1964; Parke's entry in the Hall of Fame at the National Museum of Racing, www.racingmuseum.org/hall-of-fame/horse-trainers-view.asp?varID=48; a website maintained by some of Parke's children, www.burleyparke.com; and personal communications between the author and members of the family.
35. Ivan Parke won 419 of 1,787 flat races from 1923 to 1925, 23.4 percent, http://www.racingmuseum.org/hall-of-fame/horse-jockeys-view.asp?varID=52.
36. *American Racing Manual*, 1951 edition, 304.
37. McEvoy, *Seabiscuit Story*, 126; "Obituary of Red Pollard," *Blood-Horse*, March 21, 1981.
38. National Museum of Racing and Fall of Fame, http://www.racingmuseum.org/hall-of-fame/horse-jockeys-view.asp?varID=74.
39. Beckwith, *Longden Legend*, 27.
40. Curley Grieve, "65,000 Fans Roar Tribute to Longden," *San Francisco Examiner*, February 26, 1950.
41. Mary Simon, "Twist of Fate spared Longden from *Titanic* Disaster," *Thoroughbred Times*, April 14, 2012, http://www.thoroughbredtimes.com/national-news/2012/04/14/a-simple-twist-of-fate.aspx.
42. Stephanie Diaz, "Back on Track," *Sports Illustrated*, July 11, 1994.
43. Beckwith, *Longden Legend*, 12.

Chapter 3

44. Peter and Hull, *Peter Principle*.
45. Handicaps should be distinguished from weight-for-age, or scale weight, races. The Kentucky Derby, for example, is run under weight-for-age conditions. The "scale" for three-year-olds racing in May is 126 pounds for males and 121 pounds for fillies, and every horse in the Derby carries the scale weight, regardless of ability (or lack thereof).
46. *Thoroughbred Champions*, 106, 122.

47. Paul Lowry, "Ponder Idle as Citation, Noor Drill for San Juan," *Los Angeles Times*, March 3, 1950.
48. Robert Hebert, "Review of a Successful Meeting: The San Juan Was the Top Race," *Blood-Horse*, March 18, 1950, 624.
49. Ibid.
50. Robert Burns, "To a Mouse," stanza 7. The lines are often quoted in proverb form: "The best laid plans of mice and men often go awry."
51. Abe Kemp, "Citation Launches Comeback at Santa Anita Today!" *Daily Racing Form*, January 11, 1950.
52. Ibid.
53. Bowen, *Masters of the Turf*, 272.
54. Oscar Otis, "Citation Gets Top Weight for Saturday's 'Cap," *San Francisco Chronicle*, February 8, 1950.
55. Abe Kemp, "All Calumet! Ponder Edges Citation," *San Francisco Examiner*, February 12, 1950.
56. Hillenbrand, *Seabiscuit*, 173–81.
57. Curley Grieve, "Howard Hopeful for Noor; Longden Guns for Two Lea," *San Francisco Examiner*, February 25, 1950.

Chapter 4

58. Beckwith, *Longden Legend*, 30.
59. Ibid.
60. Maurice Bernard, "Brooks, Calumet Rider, Has Narrow Escape as Horse Bolts, Throws Him," *San Francisco Examiner*, February 22, 1950.
61. Oscar Otis, "Crowd at Handicap," *San Francisco Chronicle*, February 26, 1950.
62. Eddie Arcaro remains the only rider to win two Triple Crowns, although jockey Ron Turcotte came close with Meadow Stable's Riva Ridge (winner of the Derby and Preakness in 1972) and Secretariat (winner of the 1973 Triple Crown).
63. Maurice Bernard, "Gilbert on Ponder in 100 G," *San Francisco Examiner*, February 21, 1950.
64. Kent Hollingsworth, longtime editor of the *Blood-Horse*, commented that Kayak II finished a "restrained second by a half-length." McEvoy, *Seabiscuit Story*, 117; "Seabiscuit (58th in a series on The Great Ones," *Blood-Horse*, April 18, 1970.

65. A bettor with a win ticket collects only if the selected horse wins the race, a bet to place pays if the horse finishes first or second and a bet to show pays if the horse runs first, second or third.
66. Paul Lowry, "Jones Nixes Heavy Imposts on Citation," *Los Angeles Times*, February 27, 1950.
67. Georgeff, *Citation*, 161–62.
68. Paul Zimmerman, "Noor Defeats Citation in Stretch Drive," *Los Angeles Times*, February 26, 1950.
69. Beckwith, *Longden Legend*, 67.
70. The Longden interview was an excerpt taken from *In Pursuit of Greatness*, a 1987 film produced by Joe Burnham. The segment was restored and edited by Edward Kip Hannan, who works in the Television Department at Betfair Hollywood Park.
71. Curley Grieve, "65,000 Fans Roar Tribute to Longden," *San Francisco Examiner*, February 26, 1950.
72. Robertson, *History of Thoroughbred Racing in America*, 428.

Chapter 5

73. Santa Anita racing secretary Webb Everett, referring to the 1950 San Juan Capistrano Handicap. Georgeff, *Citation*, 164.
74. Paul Lowry, "Ponder Idle as Citation, Noor Drill for San Juan," *Los Angeles Times*, March 3, 1950.
75. Hirsch and Plowden, *In the Winner's Circle*, 95–97.
76. Paul Lowry, "Jones Nixes Heavy Imposts on Citation," *Los Angeles Times*, February 27, 1950.
77. Evan Shipman, "Jones Says Citation Ran One of His Top Races in Santa Anita," *Daily Racing Form*, February 28, 1950.
78. Ibid.
79. Ibid.
80. Hirsch and Plowden, *In the Winner's Circle*, 97.
81 Georgeff, *Citation*, 164.
82. Robert Hebert, "Review of a Successful Meeting," *Blood-Horse*, March 18, 1950, 624–26.
83. H.A. Jones, "The Best I Ever Saw," September 5, 2001, http://www.bloodhorse.com/horse-racing/articles/5707/the-best-i-ever-saw#ixzz20MEwKaQk.

84. Alvarado, *Untold Story of Joe Hernandez*.
85. Bowen, *At the Wire*.
86. Paul Lowry, "Howard Horse Breaks Record," *Los Angeles Times*, March 5, 1950; Maurice Bernard, "Noor Again! Citation Fails by Nose," *San Francisco Examiner*, March 5, 1950.
87. *San Francisco Chronicle*, "Longden: Toughest I've Ever Ridden," March 5, 1950.
88. Lowry, "Howard Horse Breaks Record."
89. Hirsch and Plowden, *In the Winner's Circle*, 98.
90. Darold Fredericks, "Tanforan Race Track's History," *Daily Journal*, July 6, 2009.
91. Prescott Sullivan, "The Low Down," *San Francisco Examiner*, April 7, 1950.
92. Executive Order No. 9066, signed by President Roosevelt on February 19, 1942, gave the military sweeping power to exclude any citizen from coastal areas stretching from Southern California north to Washington and to relocate individuals deemed to be threats to national security. The law was upheld by the Supreme Court of the United States in *Korematsu v. United States*, 323 U.S. 214 (1944). Kermit L. Hall, ed., *The Oxford Guide to the Supreme Court* (New York: Oxford University Press, Inc., 2005), 561–62.
93. *San Francisco Examiner*, "Match Race Is Rejected," March 8, 1950.
94. Abe Kemp, "Citation Out of Tanfo 50 Grander," *San Francisco Examiner*, April 13, 1950.
95. Pete Pedersen, "Too Great a Risk to Let Noor Race," *San Francisco Chronicle*, April 23, 1950.
96. Pete Pedersen, "Tanfo 'Cap Tomorrow; Shoemaker Wins Pair," *San Francisco Chronicle*, April 21, 1950.
97. Abe Kemp, "Here's Why Howard Scratched Noor," *San Francisco Examiner*, April 23, 1950.
98. "Obituary of Burley Parke," *Blood-Horse* (October 17, 1977), 4882.
99. Kemp, "Here's Why Howard Scratched Noor."

Chapter 6

100. Abe Kemp, "Noor, Citation Train Well for June 3 Stakes," *San Francisco Examiner*, May 10, 1950.

101. Pete Pedersen, "Irish-Bred May Pass Up Mile Run," *San Francisco Chronicle*, May 24, 1950.
102. Georgeff, *Citation*, 167.
103. Ibid., 168.
104. Oscar Otis, "Albany Today-Citation vs. Noor," *San Francisco Chronicle*, June 17, 1950.
105. Oscar Otis, "Citation, Noor Race Set Saturday," *San Francisco Chronicle*, June 15, 1950.
106. *Daily Racing Form*, "Noor Now Holder of World Record," June 20, 1950.
107. Abe Kemp, "Noor Beats Citation, Sets Record," *San Francisco Examiner*, June 18, 1950.
108. Ibid.
109. Ibid.
110. *Los Angeles Times*, "Big Cy Given Break in Weights," June 21, 1950.
111. Abe Kemp, "Noor Wins—Cracks World Record," *San Francisco Examiner*, June 25, 1950.
112 Oscar Otis, "Noor Does It Again—Record Time," *San Francisco Chronicle* (June 25, 1950).
113. Kemp, "Noor Wins."
114. Hirsch and Plowden, *In the Winner's Circle*, 100.
115. Ibid., 102–03.
116. Personal communication with the author.
117. Robertson, *History of Thoroughbred Racing in America*, 431.
118. Ibid., 430.
119. Kemp, "Noor Wins."

Chapter 7

120. *Los Angeles Times*, "Trainer Holds Noor for Big American 'Cap," July 11, 1950.
121. Maurice Bernard, "Noor Roars to Close Win in $50,000 'Cap," *San Francisco Examiner*, July 23, 1950.
122. *San Francisco Chronicle*, "Three Races for Noor—Then Stud," July 19, 1950.
123. Bernard, "Noor Roars to Close Win."
124. Joe H. Palmer, *American Race Horses 1950* (New York: A.S. Barnes and Company, 1951), 45.

125. Abe Kemp, "Parke Says: Noor to Go," *San Francisco Examiner*, June 23, 1950.
126. Hillenbrand, *Seabiscuit*, 110.
127. Robertson, *History of Thoroughbred Racing in America*, 431.
128. Abe Kemp, "Noor Coming Back to Coast for Rest," *San Francisco Examiner*, October 11, 1950.
129. Will Connolly, "Noor Rated Greatest Importation to U.S. Turf Since Phar Lap," *San Francisco Chronicle*, December 11, 1950.
130. Palmer, *American Race Horses 1950*, 45.
131. Ibid.
132. Bowen, *Legacies of the Turf*, 36.
133. Attributed to Yogi Berra, who was commenting on back-to-back home runs hit by New York Yankee players Mickey Mantle and Roger Maris during the early 1960s.
134. Oscar Otis, "Noor Rockets at Hollypark," *San Francisco Chronicle*, December 2, 1950.
135. "*Noor Wins the Gold Cup, Sets Another Track Record," *Blood-Horse*, December 16, 1950, 1368.
136. Abe Kemp, "Noor Flashes to $102,100 Triumph!" *San Francisco Examiner*, December 10, 1950.
137. Robert Hebert, "*Noor & Parke Exit Together, but the Trainer Will Return," *Blood-Horse*, December 23, 1950), 1432.
138. Ibid.
139. Robertson, *History of Thoroughbred Racing in America*, 432.
140. Ibid.
141. Ibid.

Chapter 8

142. *San Francisco Chronicle*, "Noor Calls It Quits," December 15, 1950.
143. *Horse Racing's Top 100 Moments*, 94.
144. The Average-Earnings Index was developed by the late Joe Estes when he was editor of the *Blood-Horse* magazine as a statistical tool to compare the earnings of horses sired by one stallion with the earnings of all horses racing during the same period of time. For a more complete explanation, see "Fast Facts—What Is the Average-Earnings Index (AEI) in Thoroughbred Breeding?" April 21, 2009, http://cs.bloodhorse.

com/blogs/scot/archive/2009/04/21/fast-facts-what-is-the-average-earnings-index-aei-in-thoroughbred-breeding.aspx.
145. Milton Toby's *Dancer's Image: The Forgotten Story of the 1968 Kentucky Derby* (Charleston, SC: The History Press, 2011) is the only authoritative investigation into the Dancer's Image controversy.
146. "Late Items," *Blood-Horse* (November 25, 1974), 5177.

Chapter 9

147. The recounting of the dig at Loma Rica Ranch on August 26, 2011, is based on numerous personal communications with several of those individuals in attendance, including Charlotte Farmer, Erin Dwyer, Denise Jaffke and Gary Parke.
148. The tendency of bone to stick to the tongue is an identifying peculiarity associated with the fact that bone, unlike rock or fossilized wood, is porous and absorbs saliva.
149. Set apart here, and throughout the remainder of this book, are the recollections of Charlotte Farmer, provided at the request of the author. Unless otherwise indicated, details of the search for Noor, negotiations with city planners and developers and the trip across country with Noor's remains are based on these recollections.
150. When the *Blood-Horse* ranked the best Thoroughbreds of the twentieth century, Kelso was fourth behind only Man o' War, Secretariat and Citation. *Thoroughbred Champions*, 22–25.
151. Hillenbrand is author of the bestseller *Seabiscuit: An American Legend*.
152. Seal was referring to a brief reference to Noor in Laura Hillenbrand's book identifying the horse as Charles Howard's "one last success on the track." Hillebrand, *Seabiscuit*, 338.
153. *Union*, "MacBoyle Track to Be Restored as Equine Park," May 9, 2008, http://www.theunion.com/article/20080509/NEWS/946302319&parentprofile=search.
154. Cheri March, "New Urbanism Arrives in Gold Country," *Placer Sentinel*, June 12, 2009, 2.
155. "Cultural Resources," *City of Grass Valley 2020 General Plan*, 13–4.
156. F.W. Koester, "Loma Rica," *Thoroughbred of California* (April 1968), 656.

157. Trina Kleist, "Loma Rica Enviro Review OK, Project Moves Forward," *Union*, February 24, 2011, http://www.theunion.com/article/20110224/NEWS/110229855&parentprofile=search.
158. "Loma Rica Ranch Specific Plan," No. SP 07PLN-49, Approved May 2011, 3–13.
159. Ibid.
160. Jack Shinar, "Hollywood Park Plans to Race Through 2011," *Blood Horse*, August 7, 2010, http://www.bloodhorse.com/horse-racing/articles/58272/hollywood-park-plans-to-race-through-2011.
161. http://betfairhollywoodpark.com/about-history.
162. Zenyatta's "official" Facebook page is extremely popular, with more than 110,000 "likes" through the first half of 2012, https://www.facebook.com/#!/ZenyattaOfficial.

Chapter 10

163. Interview with Michael Blowen, July 6, 2012.

Sources

Alvarado, Rudolph Valier. *The Untold Story of Joe Hernandez: The Voice of Santa Anita*. Kindle ed. Ann Arbor, MI: Caballo Press of Ann Arbor, 2008.
American Racing Manual. Triangle Publications, 1951, 1952.
Baerlein, Richard. *Shergar and the Aga Khan's Thoroughbred Empire*. London: Michael Joseph Ltd., 1984.
Beckwith, B.K. *The Longden Legend*. Santa Anita ed. Cranbury, NJ: A.S. Barnes and Co., Inc., 1976.
Blood-Horse
Bowen, Edward L. *At the Wire: Horse Racing's Greatest Moments*. Kindle ed. Lexington, KY: Eclipse Press, 2001.
———. *Legacies of the Turf: A Century of Great Thoroughbred Breeders*. Vol. 2. Lexington, KT: Eclipse Press, 2004.
———. *Masters of the Turf: Ten Trainers Who Dominated Horse Racing's Golden Age*. Lexington, KY: Eclipse Press, 2007.
Burns, Robert. "To a Mouse." 1786.
Daily Racing Form
Dodson, James. *American Triumvirate: Sam Snead, Byron Nelson, Ben Hogan, and the Modern Age of Golf*. New York: Alfred A. Knopf, 2012.
Georgeff, Phil. *Citation: In a Class by Himself*. Boulder, CO: Taylor Trade Publishing, 2003.
Hewitt, Abram S. *Sires Lines*. Updated ed. Lexington, KY: Eclipse Press, 2006.
Hillenbrand, Laura. *Seabiscuit: An American Legend*. New York: Random House, 2001.

Hirsch, Joe, and Gene Plowden. *In the Winner's Circle: The Jones Boys of Calumet Farm*. New York: Mason & Lipscomb, 1974.

Horse Racing's Greatest Rivalries. Lexington, KY: Eclipse Press, 2008.

Horse Racing's Top 100 Moments. Lexington, KY: Eclipse Press, 2006.

Jodidio, Philip. *A Racing and Breeding Tradition: The Horses of the Aga Khan*. New York: Prestel USA, 2011.

Landers, A.T. *Professional Care of the Racehorse*. Lexington, KY: Eclipse Press, 2006.

Los Angeles Times

McEvoy, John, ed. *The Seabiscuit Story*. Lexington, KY: Eclipse Press, 2003.

Palmer, Joe H. *American Race Horses 1950*. New York: A.S. Barnes and Company, 1951.

Peter, Laurence J., and Raymond Hull. *The Peter Principle: Why Things Always Go Wrong*. New York: William Morrow and Co., 1969.

Robertson, William H.P. *The History of Thoroughbred Racing in America*. Englewood Cliffs, NJ: Prentice-Hall, Inc., 1964.

San Francisco Chronicle

San Francisco Examiner

Sidorsky, Robert. *Golf 365 Days: A History*. New York: Abrams, 2008.

Smith, Pohla. *Citation, Thoroughbred Legends, No. 3*. Lexington, KY: Eclipse Press, 2000.

Thoroughbred Champions: Top 100 Racehorses of the 20th Century. Lexington, KY: Blood-Horse, 1999.

Thoroughbred Record

Thoroughbred Times

About the Author

Milt Toby is an author and attorney who has been writing about Thoroughbred racing for some forty years. His six previous books include *Dancer's Image: The Forgotten Story of the 1968 Kentucky Derby* (also from The History Press), which won the Dr. Tony Ryan Book Award as the best book about Thoroughbred racing published in 2011 and an American Horse Publications Editorial Award for the best equine book of 2011. Milt is a director of American Horse Publications and a former chair of the Kentucky Bar Association's Equine Law Section. He lives in Central Kentucky with his wife, Roberta, two dogs and two cats. Visit his website at www.miltonctoby.com.

Visit us at
www.historypress.net

CPSIA information can be obtained
at www.ICGtesting.com
Printed in the USA
LVHW081343130121
676397LV00005B/40